Power Producer

A Practical Guide to TV News Producing

by Dow Smith

PUBLISHED BY
RADIO-TELEVISION NEWS DIRECTORS ASSOCIATION
WASHINGTON, DC
1.800.80.RTNDA

ISBN 0-9678432-0-0

Copyright ©2000 Dow C. Smith

All rights reserved. No part of this book may be reproduced, stored in a retrieval system, or transmitted in any form or by any means, electronic, mechanical, photocopying, recording or otherwise without the prior written permission of the publisher.

Publisher:
Radio-Television News Directors Association
1000 Connecticut Avenue NW, Suite 615
Washington, DC 20036
Phone: 800.80.RTNDA

Cover Illustration: Ken Coffelt/Stock Illustration Source
Design: DRPollard and Associates, Inc., Arlington, VA
Printing: Prestige Paper Products, Inc., Rockville, MD

First Edition

Contents

About the Author		5
Acknowledgments		6
Introduction		7
Chapter 1:	The Producer's Roles	11
Chapter 2:	Thinking Like a Reporter	19
Chapter 3:	Where Do You Live?	25
Chapter 4:	Getting the News	31
Chapter 5:	Writing Broadcast News	39
Chapter 6:	Building the News Show	49
Chapter 7:	The Newscast Format	57
Chapter 8:	The Devil Is in the Details	63
Chapter 9:	More Than News	75
Chapter 10:	Reporting the News with Graphics	83
Chapter 11:	Teases That Sell	91
Chapter 12:	Coaching Your Team	97
Chapter 13:	Dealing with Difficult Personalities	107
Chapter 14:	Ratings & Research	115
Chapter 15:	The Law, Ethics & Your Newscast	125
Chapter 16:	You & Your Career	135
Appendix:	Resources for Producers	141
Index		147

Featuring

Producer Survey by Janice Gin	16
Producer Alice Johnson Main	23
News Director Willie Chriesman	46
Newscast Director Phil Hutchings	69
News Anchor Demetria Kalodimos	104
News Researcher Desiree Newhart Hill	123
Ethicist Bob Steele	132

About the Author

Dow Smith is an associate professor of broadcast journalism at the S.I. Newhouse School of Public Communications at Syracuse University, Syracuse, NY. He joined the Newhouse faculty in 1995. At Newhouse he teaches both broadcast journalism and television management courses. He has developed an advanced producing and news management course in conjunction with three local affiliates. In 1998, Smith was selected as teacher of the year.

Smith has almost 30 years of experience in broadcast news. After receiving a master's degree from the University of Missouri in 1969, he began as a producer at KOVR-TV in Sacramento, CA, and went on to produce at KPIX-TV in San Francisco and WBBM-TV in Chicago. He returned to KPIX in 1973 as executive producer and then did a tour as news assignment manager at what is now KCBS-TV in Los Angeles. Smith became the news director at WPLG-TV in Miami in 1976 where he worked with legendary anchor Ann Bishop and an exceptional reporting and producing staff. He went on to be news director at WJLA-TV in Washington and WDIV-TV in Detroit. He became general manager of WTEN-TV in Albany, NY, in 1987, and later was general manager of WVTM-TV in Birmingham, AL. As a news director, Smith's news departments received two DuPont awards, a Peabody, and numerous Emmy awards, including three for best newscast.

Prior to graduate school, Smith served as a Navy public information officer in Saigon where he escorted television crews into the field and wrote stories for release. His journalism roots go deep—his father was a newspaperman in San Francisco for 30 years.

In addition to teaching, Smith conducts producer workshops for the Radio and Television News Directors Foundation. He also races a 1958 Morgan sports car in vintage events in the Northeast.

Dow Smith and his wife Bonnie live in Delmar, NY.

| Dedication |

For my wife Bonnie Smith. She deserves the credit for four excellent children who survived far too many markets.

Acknowledgments

Like television news, writing a book is a team sport. It takes a lot of people to bring together a book.

Editor Pamela Stovall made this all possible because she taught an old broadcast newswriter how to construct a reasonably coherent paragraph. Her patience and humor got me through what I sometimes called "book hell."

The line illustrations inside are by Matthew D. Smith, my son, who prefers to draw comic books but spent so much of his youth in newsrooms he has a good idea of what producers look like. Also, my daughter Pauline Smith, a beginning producer, read much of the handbook to make sure it applies to someone with a liberal arts degree now producing an a.m. newscast.

This book would not have happened without the support of Barbara Cochran and Noreen Welle at Radio-Television News Directors Association. They inherited the idea but went forward with the project, for which I am grateful.

My colleagues in the Broadcast Journalism Department in the S. I. Newhouse School of Public Communications at Syracuse University played a big part in developing this handbook. First, Bob Lissit read and pre-edited much of the material, adding great questions and commentary to make the handbook better. Professors Chris Tuohey (a former producer), Barbara Fought (a former investigative producer), and Dona Hayes (a former reporter) all reviewed chapters as I went along and had excellent comments based on their professional experience and knowledge. Producers Alice Main and Ted Wilson were a major source of advice. Freelance producer Robin Briley Cowan and former producer, now consultant, Desiree Newhart Hill at AR&D also reviewed the book and had valuable comments. One-time power producer, now general manager, Steve Wasserman, also contributed ideas for the book. Dennis Kendall at Egad! reviewed the chapter on graphics and supplied samples for that chapter. Vincent Nasso at Nielsen Media Research reviewed the chapter on ratings to make sure I had the inner workings of Nielsen correct.

The faculty at The Poynter Institute, including Paul Pohlman, Valerie Hyman, Scott Libin, Jill Geisler and Bob Steele, all provided names and ideas.

Those who gave up their time and knowledge to be interviewed deserve special thanks: Willie Chriesman, Janice Gin, Desiree Newhart Hill, Phil Hutchings, Demetria Kalodimos, Alice Main and Bob Steele.

Finally, I must acknowledge the contribution of all the producers, news managers and consultants I've worked with over the years. They taught me producing and the television news business by showing how it should be done. Most have gone on to fame and fortune. It's well-deserved. I'd like to thank you all for making my life richer by being such great people.

Introduction

Television news producers are incredibly important, but most people don't know who they are or what they do. Producers have far more control over the news and how it's reported than any other individual in the newsroom, including the anchors. However, in local television and cable news, producers decide what news stories the viewers see and how the news is presented. It's the producer's call on which public issues get exposure on the news. A producer's decisions make an anchor team shine. A producer leads the teams of dedicated professionals that get the news on the air.

Among the thousands of producers working behind the scenes in television news, there is a group at the top qualified to be called "power producers." These producers have mastered all facets of producing. They make a positive impact on their newsrooms and on their communities. They create successful newscasts both in ratings and news coverage. Power producers make a difference. They are leaders in television news. Using this handbook, you too may become one of these rare and valuable power producers.

Why You Need To Read this Book

First, congratulations on your decision to become a producer. There has never been a better time to be a producer. There is a huge demand. The lack of experienced and skilled producers is a major problem.

Today, news directors hire smart people with degrees in subjects like English literature or political science and turn them into producers. This is not an easy process. There is little history of mentoring, coaching and training in broadcast journalism. To learn producing, most producers have had to tough it out on their own. They learned through watching other producers and doing the job. It's difficult to become a power producer on your own. It takes exceptional personal drive and dedication. That's why there are few power producers.

Whether you are an experienced producer or just starting out, this handbook will help you build a successful career. It provides the beginning producer with the tools he or she needs to learn the fundamentals of producing. It will help those who are just entering the television news business by providing a grounding in the principles of journalism. If you are already producing, this handbook provides a framework for you to understand your job. Not only will this handbook help you hone areas where your skills are weak, it will help you develop additional skills you need to excel as a producer. With practice and attention, and this handbook, you can join that elite band of power producers.

This Is Not a Textbook

You are looking at a handbook, not a textbook. There are no trick questions, no exercises, or even any easy true or false questions. This is a practical handbook that explains the art and practice of producing. It's designed to be accessible for those who want to use it to master their craft. It's an easy-to-use guide to television news producing with practical solutions to everyday challenges.

Who Should Read this Book

You'll find this book invaluable if...

- You're a student interested in a television news career but you know little about producing and what the job entails. You'll learn about a career you may not have heard of or thought about before.
- You're a student or a beginner who knows you want to be a producer. This handbook will get you started on your career with a sound foundation of practical knowledge.
- You're in your first or second producing job. This handbook explains in detail what you need to know about producing but probably haven't been told. It will provide answers and solutions to problems that you face every day.
- You're an experienced producer. This handbook serves as a valuable review of the craft. It will take you to that next level in your career and help keep your skills fresh.
- You're a television news professional such as an anchor, reporter or news manager with no producing experience. It will help you understand the complex profession of producing.

How This Handbook Is Organized

This handbook is organized to help you understand the full scope of the craft. Producing is a complex job involving a range of skills. And those who become power producers master a vast array of skills and knowledge. To make this concept of power producer easier to understand and master, this handbook is divided into sections. Each section covers one of the critical roles of producing. If you want to know more about a specific aspect of producing, just turn to that section.

In each section you'll find invaluable information that will make your job easier and more rewarding. There's great information on problems you face every day like dealing with difficult people and how to do a better job of using graphics in your newscast. You'll find practical tips like how to get to know a new community and how to encourage more enterprise reporting in your newsroom. Every chapter contains invaluable information producers want and need to know.

Mastering producing is only part of this handbook. You'll also find out how to land a producing job, and what to do when things aren't going well in your current newsroom. This is all practical information to help you build a successful career.

You'll also find an appendix called Resources for Producers. This appendix guides you to the material and information you need to develop as a producer.

Throughout this handbook are a series of interviews with seasoned professionals on producing. You'll hear from people at the top of their craft about how they became power producers. You'll hear from an anchor and a newscast director about how they work with producers and what you can do to build better relationships with the people who are key to your success or failure. You'll find out about news research and how to make solid ethical decisions.

Don't miss the survey on page 16 done by power producer Janice Gin of KGO-TV in San Francisco. You'll read about many of the frustrations, opinions and problems of producers. This handbook will provide answers to the frustrations and problems every producer faces.

Throughout the handbook you'll find boxes with tips and warnings based on the experience of other producers. These are the fine points and pitfalls of producing.

What Makes Me an Expert?

You may be wondering why a university professor in his fifties is writing about producing. How could someone that age, who started in television news 30 years ago, know anything about your life as a produc-

TIP
DO NOT MISS THESE

 Tips are boxed and sprinkled through the text. These tips offer great information you need to know to develop into a power producer.

WARNING!
DO NOT MISS THESE

 These boxed warnings provide critical information on issues and problems that could save your show from a major on-air disaster or save you from a careless mistake that could destroy your reputation and career.

er? It's a legitimate question, particularly given the youth of most producers.

To start with, I was one of the first graduates of the University of Missouri School of Journalism who actually wanted to be a producer. Missouri now has a strong program for producers, but 30 years ago none of the professors knew what a producer did. So I learned just like you, through on-the-job training, and by trial and error (mostly error).

Talent was an enigma even then. Nothing prepared me for my first job working with an anchorman who drank his dinner at the topless bar next door. My first "people" problem.

Over the years, as a news director, and even as a general manager, I always enjoyed sitting in on the morning meeting and visiting the control room during the newscast. When I was fed up with budget problems and corporate busywork, it was invigorating to talk to the producers because producing is the creative side of television. Frankly, for all the frustrations, producing is fun.

Admittedly, today's broadcasts are faster paced. Production is more complicated with computer still stores, computer-generated graphics, advanced character generators and satellite feeds. While a producer has to master technology, producing is still basically about being a journalist, a storyteller and a news writer, the same skills I learned 30 years ago.

The goal of this handbook is to save you from having to learn producing the old-fashioned and hard way, the way most producers have learned the craft in the past. In reading this book, you will have the knowledge you need to climb rapidly to the pinnacle of producing, to become a power producer.

Television news is always evolving. Feel free to write or e-mail if you have a comment about the handbook, or any ideas you think might help producers. E-mail me at dcsmit02@syr.edu or write to the S.I. Newhouse School of Public Communications, Syracuse University, 215 University Place, Syracuse, NY 13244. Thank you.

Dow Smith
January 2000

Chapter 1
The Producer's Roles

In This Chapter:

- What Do Producers Do?
- A Formal Job Description
- The Evolution of a Power Producer
- The Qualities of a Power Producer
- The Seven Roles of a Power Producer

Chapter 1: The Producer's Roles

> "Because today's producers have so much more responsibility, most formal job descriptions don't work."

It's a moment every producer experiences. You're at a family gathering or a neighborhood party, and someone comes up to you and asks what you do for a living. When you reply that you work in television, the person then asks the inevitable question, "Have I seen you on the air?" When you say no, you're a news producer, the person looks disappointed, having no idea what a producer does. It certainly doesn't sound important. The person drifts away, unhappy that you aren't someone famous like a news anchor.

People outside television, even some in television, have little idea just how important news producers are. However, as a producer, you play a crucial role in deciding what news the viewers see. You decide what the anchors do and say. You control the pace and flow of the newscast. You create a newscast valuable to the audience and to your station. Producing is incredibly important and increasingly complex.

Because producing as a career isn't understood, it's hard for news managers to find good producers. Few students graduate from journalism schools or communications programs with producing as a career goal. Faced with a small pool of producer applicants, news directors often hire bright people with broad life experiences and then train them as news producers.

Unfortunately, the downside of bringing in people without journalism training is that they don't understand the basics of broadcast journalism. Producers first must be journalists, and learning to be an accomplished journalist is hard work. Producing is a demanding profession and it doesn't tolerate many mistakes. A simple lapse in judgment can end your career and even make you a national laughingstock.

No matter what your background, this handbook is designed to help you avoid mistakes and build a successful producing career. Whether you need help with the basics of broadcast journalism or ideas on how to improve your tease writing, this handbook provides you with all the information you need to become a "power producer."

What is a power producer? Basically, you become a power producer when you've taken the time and personal dedication to reach the top levels of producing—it's when you've mastered all of the producer's many roles. In this chapter, you'll learn how you can become that unique and highly valued person. You'll begin your development into a power producer by defining the job. Power producers know they can't do the job unless they understand what it is. The chapter ends with a valuable framework for you to use in understanding the full scope of your job: the seven roles of a power producer.

What Do Producers Do?

The way to start learning about your job is by defining it. How would you describe your job to someone who has no idea what producing is all about? Perhaps you might say that a news producer assembles the various pieces that make up a news broadcast. Then you get that broadcast on the air... and off... on time. Along the way, you write the copy, decide which story belongs where in relation to the others, and decide how long each story runs.

Yesterday's producers. Twenty-five years ago, producers took the stories covered by the station's reporters, along with stories based on wire copy, and arranged them in some logical sequence. Producers had little say in what stories were covered, and they gave little thought to the audience or how to make the news more relevant. Their main concern was getting the film edited and the stories written. These producers still exist, and are called "stackers and packers." That's not a compliment. Stackers and packers perform only two roles: news decisions and newscast production. That concept of producing is limited.

Today's producers. Today, producers do far more. And power producers do even more. A power producer acts as journalist, news writer, production expert, promotion writer, team leader, researcher, and lawyer/ethicist.

A Formal Job Description

Because today's producers have so much more responsibility than they used to, most formal job descriptions don't work.

A producer's role can vary from newsroom to newsroom. That's one reason job descriptions don't cover all your potential roles. Why producers in your newsroom work the way they do depends on your department's structure and history. It's important that you understand how your colleagues view producing because you must work within the newsroom culture to be successful.

Talent. For example, who originally produced the news programs—the anchors or the news director? If anchors used to be in charge, they may want to continue to tell you what to put in the broadcast. If the news director was in charge, he or she may take control of the rundown, leaving you the role of production assistant instead of producer.

Reporters. Does the station have a strong reputation for being a "reporters' shop?" In some newsrooms the reporters call the shots. This may limit your ability when it comes to creating your newscast. You may not have much flexibility in assigning story length and story order.

Unions. Although it is uncommon, some producers are unionized. This tends to be the case

---

SAMPLE JOB DESCRIPTION

This is a formal job description from a major-market television station, part of a large station group. It focuses on the mechanics of producing and covers some of the supervisory roles that producers handle.

A. Identification

Job title or classification: News Producer
Immediate supervisor's title: Executive Producer
Department.: News

B. Responsibilities

1. Direct content, production, writing and execution of assigned newscast and news updates.
2. Direct and supervise the work of news anchors, including weather and sports.
3. Direct and supervise reporters and assignment editor.
4. Write, direct and supervise writers assigned to newscast. Review scripts.
5. Accurately communicate with the director to ensure the cleanest on-air product.
6. Ensure that all videotape is ready for air.
7. Select appropriate graphic and pre-production for best story presentation.
8. Perform other tasks as assigned by the executive producer.

C. Special Skills

1. Ability to make difficult decisions under pressure.
2. Strong leadership skills and the ability to motivate staff.
3. Excellent editorial judgment and writing skills.
4. Strong organizational skills.

in a few stations and in the largest markets. If you are in a union, then you are limited in what you can do. You may be working for an executive producer from management who has the final say. Even if you aren't in a union, in large markets you may work with unionized writers. You won't be able to write copy, only edit it.

The Evolution of a Power Producer

Precisely defining the producer job also is difficult because producers evolve during their careers. That evolution begins almost immediately. Remember that it's impossible to graduate from any college journalism program as a power producer. You need daily experience in newsgathering and in the news production process. You can liken this need for real-world experience in broadcast journalism to the residency physicians must complete after medical school.

For example, you can't really appreciate the coordination and logistics it takes to get a big breaking news story on the air until you've done it. Imagine this scenario: A passenger jet crashes. You're alone in the newsroom producing the morning newscast, and you need to know exactly how to respond: how to get a bulletin on the air, whom to call in, where to send the live trucks and crews, and how to deal with all the networks and stations calling for tape or a live report. This isn't covered in a course or a textbook.

There are four stages of producing (see box). So if you are just starting, you must serve a residency as a beginning producer. You work through progressive stages before earning the unique status of power producer. And even if you have produced for a while, you still are evolving toward becoming a power producer. Where are you on the path?

The Qualities of a Power Producer

Once producers have progressed to the power producer stage, they share common professional skills and qualities. Think about the best producers you work with now. Watch how they conduct themselves during the news process.

As you watch these producers in action, you'll notice that power producers share at least five special traits: presence, command, organization, passion and decisiveness.

Presence. Power producers have presence,

THE FOUR STAGES OF PRODUCING

After watching hundreds of producers develop during my career as a producer, news director and general manager, it's clear to me that producers go through four distinct stages. Of course, as in any progression, the lines between the different levels are imprecise.

Stage One: Scared to Death. At the first stage, the primary concern is just getting the newscast off the air on time. Who cares if the story flow doesn't make sense or weather was cut by 30 seconds, leaving out the forecast? The producer made it off on time. This is the white-knuckle or computer-hugger period that takes place when someone has just started. At this level, the beginning producer really is just trying to come to grips with the complexity of getting a newscast on and off the air.

Stage Two: The Mechanic. This is perhaps the largest group of producers. These are the stackers and packers. They can get the show off on time and assemble a clean-looking broadcast, but with the format dictated from above. At this stage, most producers are afraid to break the format. Heaven help them if a big story breaks. They won't know what to do because they're lost without the format rules. Mechanics seldom know much about the community, and they spend a good deal of time thinking about their next

and other people in the newsroom pay attention to the way they go about their job. When they say something or make a decision, people listen and respond. Other producers seek out their advice. Power producers command respect and are looked up to by the newsroom team. Presence doesn't mean being an attention-getting dresser with red suspenders or a red power blazer. Producers earn their impact on the newsroom based on skill, ability and the way they work with others, not clothing and style. You, too, can create presence in the newsroom by the way you work with other people, and by being fair, open and honest. Communicate clearly, make good decisions and keep your cool. Presence is built by these and dozens of other traits that add up over time.

Command. When power producers speak, news teams swing into action. This is because power producers have earned respect. If you've been right before and won the team's approval, they'll do what you ask. However, you lose that respect and the abili-

job, trying to move up in market size. Their management skills are primitive, and they provide little leadership. Actually, they are often anxious and tense and have a hard time working with others. The mechanic just masters the mechanics of the news process and that's all.

Stage Three: The Journeyman. These are skilled craftspeople who travel from job to job earning a living. Unfortunately, this group is second only to the mechanic in numbers, and they're common even in major-market news departments. They don't produce shows with creativity or flair, but are reliable and hard-working, and they won't get the station in legal trouble. These producers know the mechanics and something about the community, but they aren't really involved. Their organization skills are good, and they don't often show anxiety. They have enough management skills to get others to work reasonably well together. However, journeymen have a hard time thinking "outside the box," a favorite news director cliché for creativity. Unfortunately, these producers also won't ask others to do anything new or challenging. They aren't leaders.

Stage Four: The Power Producer. This is the highest level of producing, and it's difficult to find. Unfortunately, just when a producer shows any of the traits of a true power producer, he or she is often promoted to executive producer.

ty to get things done if you ask your team to do something ill-conceived or unethical.

Organization. Even beginning producers recognize the need for organization, but power producers master organization and move through the daily news production process with ease. They manage their time well and take care of tasks promptly, with a minimum of fuss.

Passion. Power producers have a passion for news. Their dedication to news is always near the surface. You see that passion in their story ideas and knowledge about current events. It's also evident in the decisions they make as they build the rundown. They come in without being called when there's a big story. They want to be part of getting the story on the air and are willing to do anything to help the newsroom.

Decisiveness. Power producers make decisions. They don't hesitate. They understand that a clear sense of direction and purpose may be more important than being perfect. It's better to make the wrong decision than no decision. At one station, an indecisive producer always led his rundown with a story entitled "TBA" (to be announced) because he was always waiting for a better lead. Hardly a decisive way to build a newscast.

The Seven Roles of a Power Producer

Power producers develop these common traits because they realize all the demands of producing. Producing is not a list of things to get done every day. Producing is about the different roles a producer plays in creating and executing a news program. Think about your day and what you accomplish. Every task you do fits within one of these seven basic producing roles:

- Journalist
- News writer
- Production expert
- Promotion writer
- Team leader
- Researcher
- Lawyer/ethicist

Power producers take these roles and make them part of who they are. They learn each role through hard work, experience and perseverance. You become a power producer once you master each role. Take a closer look at each role and think about how vital it is to quality producing.

Journalist. Power producers are first-class journalists and reporters. They have a professional drive to inform viewers about their world. Producers at this level think like reporters, have their own news sources and are in touch with the community. As journalists, power producers deliver on the promise to provide accurate, fair and balanced reporting. They demonstrate this role as they build their rundown and develop enterprise stories.

News writer. Power producers are excellent broadcast news writers. They write for the ear and understand how to match video, sound and words

TIP
SCREAMERS, PROFANITY AND CONFUSION

There's a macho idea in some newsrooms that you have to yell at people or belittle them to get something done. In television, these people are called screamers. They only add to the confusion, particularly when something goes wrong. Power producers develop an ability to stay calm and focused, even in high-stress situations. They set an example.

to tell a story. While some producers slip into clichés and non-conversational writing, power producers don't fall into that trap. They know their viewers and know how to command the viewer's attention and interest. They can sell a story.

Production expert. Power producers master the mechanics and showmanship of television production. How do you know you're in command of production? It can be little things—like looking at a rundown and realizing a script time is missing, or knowing just how long it takes a tape editor to get a new lead story done. Power producers know how to manage their own time and how to manage the complex production process. If you aren't comfortable with the technical side of producing, it's difficult to become a power producer.

Promotion writer. Writing teases that hook viewers and get them to stay to the end of your newscast is only part of what you need to know about promotion. Power producers understand the importance of teases and how this daily task is tied to the station's promotion and marketing. They also understand that a good tease is journalistically accurate and doesn't mislead the audience.

Team leader. Although this title isn't in job descriptions, leadership is essential to developing into a power producer. A power producer leads a team. It takes dozens of people from different departments to get a newscast on the air. Power producers have the ability to draw out the best from others on the team. This means working

The Producer Survey
A Survey of Local TV Newscast Producers: Their Wishes and Wants

Janice Gin
Executive Producer
KGO-TV
San Francisco

At times, producers have the feeling that no one else understands or shares their problems. This survey indicates that you are not alone. Most producers share the same experiences. For instance, there is little formal job training. News directors aren't good about coaching and feedback, and "people problems" are a major headache. But in the end, producers get a tremendous creative lift out of the job.

As you go through this handbook, you will find answers to most of the producer concerns identified in this survey. You'll learn how to get past your lack of training, how to deal with people on and off the air, how to stay involved in your community, and how to make producing even more fun and more rewarding by evolving into a power producer.

In 1997, Janice Gin conducted a survey of local television newscast producers. Gin, executive producer at KGO-TV in San Francisco, conducted this informal research while preparing to be a visiting faculty member at The Poynter Institute. She wanted to know what producers need and want from their newsrooms and news managers, so they can do their jobs better.

What follows is a representative sample of the responses of two dozen producers from across the country. The participants had different amounts of experience and came from various market sizes.

Gin Asked Fellow Producers:

Looking back to when you first became a producer, what would you want management to tell you or teach you to make your job easier and your performance better?

■ Clearly define

with an attitude of mutual respect and creating a positive environment.

Researcher. How can you communicate with your viewers if you don't understand how they live their lives and what they expect from television news? To successfully present the news needed by the audience, you must develop an accurate mental picture of the audience. This is tough to do for many reasons, so you need to research your audience.

Lawyer/ethicist. A power producer has the experience to know what kind of story could present legal problems, and what kind of story raises ethical issues that could embarrass the station and damage credibility. Power producers recognize a problem story and know when to call in the news director or the lawyers or when to kill a story because of ethical concerns.

Mastering all seven roles of producing is power producing. Now that you know the basic framework of producing and journalism, you've completed the first step to becoming a power producer. You also know how power producers evolve and how they do their job. To be successful, you need to make this framework the basis for your own career.

In the next chapter, we'll tackle a more practical side of your job, getting the news and getting it on the air. This is the first and most important role of a power producer, that of journalist and reporter.

---

expectations.
- Explain news director's philosophy.
- Give me feedback on what management likes or dislikes.
- Explain the target audience.
- Tell me what they want. Be consistent. Don't tell me it's my show and then at every turn challenge and change my decisions.
- Teach everyone in the newsroom that the newscast is a team product.
- You can't do the show alone, and you depend on others who might not always come through.
- Producing is as much managing people as it is managing the news.
- Ninety-nine percent of the battle is making your anchor happy.
- What segments or talent are "sacred?"
- Explain the relationship between producers and anchors and producers and reporters. Also, explain how to get the anchors more involved in the newscasts and how to give them feedback and guidance.
- Ratings are the real story, not the well-being of the community.
- Recognize a job well done; a pat on the back is nice.
- Emphasize storytelling.
- Learn how to handle pressure in the booth and how to make decisions under pressure.

Describe how you learned your job as a producer. Who were the people who were the most helpful in this process? What made them so?

- I taught myself by observing other producers. They also gave me advice and ideas about what to do, but trial and error was the most effective way to learn producing.
- Observed other producers. One in particular was well-rounded with knowledge about the community, news events, history and journalism. He set a good example.
- News director shared his philosophy during one-on-one sessions.
- Casual comments from the news director during the newscast.
- Learned writing from other writers in the newsroom.
- Anchors provided direction by telling me what they needed in order to do their jobs.
- Sink or swim method of learning by doing.
- I learned by doing 10 shows a week for three years.

Now that you have been producing for a while, what areas do you feel you still need to improve on?

- Writing.
- Tease writing.
- Learning the market/community.
- Communicating with colleagues.
- Interpersonal skills—how not to be abrupt with people.
- More creativity with graphics and animation.
- Understanding the lead-in audience.
- Not internalizing stories that are close to me.
- Patience with reporters.
- Dealing with management. How to deal

with a lot of cooks in the kitchen.
- Time to look for memorable moment opportunities.

As a producer, what is your biggest complaint about your job?

- Managers who micromanage.
- Managers who call into the booth during the newscast asking questions about what they just saw and didn't like.
- Managers who make changes without understanding the circumstances of the moment or the background.
- Management's lack of understanding of simple physics, specifically the space-time continuum. You can only put so many stories, breakout elements, and graphics in the space of one newscast.
- Working with reporters, especially young reporters.
- Executive producers not backing producers, not taking an interest in the day-to-day issues, not pitching in to help (i.e., write a script), siding or giving in to the anchor over the producer.
- Reluctance of others to do new or different things.
- Not enough time to do everything I want done in the newscast—to think about graphic designs, full-screen text and other production values and to tweak scripts.
- Co-workers with bad attitudes.
- News can be depressing, especially bad news stories such as murders, fires and accidents.
- Long days.
- Not a great salary.
- Not enough support staff. Managers need to ask if we have enough help to allow us time to think about the content and presentation of the newscast.
- Never get an opportunity to be in the community. Most producers lose touch with the people they write about.
- Anchors do so little for so much pay and credit.

What is the one thing that you like most about being a news producer?

- It's fun.
- Making things flow.
- Seizing creative opportunities.
- Every day is different. Challenge to be creative when there's "no news."
- Crafting the newscast and seeing it come to life on the air. Seeing what you wrote on paper turn out the way you wanted it to look on the air.
- The excitement that comes when juggling several different things at once during the show and then seeing it come off without a hitch.
- Writing and seeing the vision of the newscast on paper become reality.
- Making an impact. Developing and presenting stories that affect people and community issues.
- The power to help shape the mentality of the viewers as it relates to certain issues.
- Doing good stories that have a positive impact on the community. Brave enough to not do what everyone else is doing that day.

As a producer, what keeps you motivated?

- Working with good reporters and anchors.
- A fair manager, someone who understands.
- Knowing that I can make a difference in society/community. I can have an impact on people's lives.
- I can help viewers see their community, country and the world in a realistic manner that makes their lives richer.
- Every day is a new day.
- The idea of creating a different newscast every day.
- Having the opportunity every day to tell a fabulous story.
- Wanting to be the best.
- Being the first to know. Being part of the big story.
- When there is a "win" every day.
- My family—and knowing that I have a peaceful place to come to every night.
- Paycheck.

Other comments:

- Want more input into manager's decision on what will be placed in my broadcast, specifically rating-period stories.
- Training workshops are very important but often seem to be overlooked. Managers have to make the time.
- Value the experience of others on the staff. There's a wealth of knowledge.

Chapter 2
Role One: Journalist

Thinking Like a Reporter

In This Chapter:

- What Is Journalism?
- Developing as a Journalist
- How Do You Gain General Knowledge?
- How a Power Producer Keeps Informed
- How the World Works
- The Producer as Reporter

Chapter 2:
Thinking Like a Reporter

"As a producer you've got to tell your viewers why these stories are important and how these events affect their lives."

You've probably witnessed a situation like this one in a morning news meeting. In the middle of a discussion on possible lead stories a producer pops up with, "What indictment?" The assignment editor is forced to waste time bringing the producer up to speed on an important story, such as "Feds Indict Mayor for Bribery." Certainly, it's a story the producer should have read about in the morning paper, seen on the early morning news, or heard on the radio on the way to work. How can news producers do their jobs if they don't know the news?

Power producers are first-class journalists. They think and act like journalists. They understand that keeping up with the daily news is part of producing and part of being a journalist. Even if you're new to journalism or don't have a journalism degree, there are steps you can take. You can learn how to stay on top of the news and develop the skills of a reporter.

To become a power producer, you must understand what journalism is, and this chapter supplies the information. You'll discover how to keep yourself informed on daily events and how to bring yourself up to speed on general knowledge. You need this background to make good news decisions. Background adds context and perspective to your newscasts. It makes the news valuable to your viewers. And you must know the background behind daily events to be a power producer.

But first, what is journalism, and why is it so important?

What Is Journalism?

The audience comes to a news program first for the news. Yes, viewers watch for other reasons, such as to hear the weather forecast or see what your anchors are wearing, but first they want to know about the events of the day. So as a producer, you need a solid definition of news and journalism.

One of the difficulties in defining journalism is that we don't have a consensus definition. There may be as many definitions as there are dictionaries. Journalism begins with reporting, getting the facts of a news story. As a news producer and journalist, you must be able to gather the facts and report stories.

However, journalism is more than getting information. Journalism includes writing and editing. So a simple definition of journalism is "reporting, writing and editing the news for publication or broadcast." Nevertheless, to define journalism as only reporting, writing and editing is too simple. Good journalism is more than just getting the facts and getting them on the air. As a producer you've got to tell your viewers why these stories are important and how these events affect their lives. Because you are a journalist, you add context, perspective and history to reporting, writing and editing. This is a better definition of journalism.

How do you become a first-class journalist and not just someone covering a news story? Fortunately, you will develop the makeup of a journalist as you work on becoming a power producer, because power producers are journalists.

Developing as a Journalist

Certain journalistic characteristics, or skills, are common to power producers, and you need to develop those traits.

The news junkie. First, power producers are news junkies. News junkies are people who love news and information. They have a hunger and passion for news. News is in their blood. The best newsrooms are filled with news junkies. What happens when there's a breaking story? They want to be first to the story. Later, they watch intently to see how each station does in its coverage. They want to know who had the best pictures and the most accurate information. They're highly competitive people.

General knowledge. The other trait that journalists and power producers share is that they have a body of general knowledge and information about the world and how it works. How do you know a story is important? Where does it belong in the rundown? Do you have the background information you need to sell a story to the viewers? These are some of the reasons why you need as much background knowledge as possible.

The knowledge challenge. If you don't have this basic knowledge you're liable to make serious errors in news judgment. Bad news decisions and ignorance will cost you the trust of the newsroom and the news managers. Far worse, if you allow bad information on the air, something you should have known, the station's credibility is damaged. If the viewers don't believe they can trust your news, then they won't watch! You face this knowledge challenge every day as a producer. For example, when Frank Sinatra died, you needed to know how to handle the story. He wasn't popular with the twenty-something age group, the age of beginning producers. And he no longer performed. However, even if you weren't a fan, you needed to understand that Sinatra's death was a lead story. You also needed to know things about Sinatra. You had to know something of his career, his movies and his marriages. You needed to know about rumors of a tie to organized crime. All this information needed to be in the stories about his death. This was not one of those stories where you could be forgiven for a lack of knowledge.

Jeopardy. Think of yourself as a contestant on "Jeopardy." One day you may be faced with trying to answer the "Daily Double" question from a Sinatra category, and the next day a question about cancer. You may not be a real expert in much besides TV news, but you must know about a lot of different subjects. Producers are often called "a mile wide but an inch deep" when it comes to information.

How Do You Gain General Knowledge?

In the words of one news director friend, "Read, read, read." What happens when you don't read? He tells the story of a producer who didn't know about the novel based on the Clinton campaign, "Primary Colors."

It became a major news story when the media tried to identify the anonymous author. The novel seemed so true to the scandals around President Clinton that the national media were full of speculation about the author. Who imagined that this novel itself would become an ongoing news story? Certainly not that producer.

"Read, read, read" is simple but excellent advice. Reading is the best way to get the background information you need to do your job. Reading all kinds of magazines, books, newspapers and web sites will start your knowledge base. In fact, reading every day to keep informed about current news is the best way to improve your personal knowledge base.

How a Power Producer Keeps Informed

Trying to stay up with what's happening in the world is hard work unless you're totally addicted to news. Early in your producing career you may have to force yourself to devote the time and energy needed to keep on top of the news. Then, once you understand how important being a news junkie is to your job, you become obsessed with the news.

Set a goal for yourself. Become the best-informed producer in your newsroom. Here's how you can begin to keep yourself on top:

Newspapers. Read daily newspapers and lots of them. Read five or six newspapers before work. You need to skim the national newspapers, including *The New York Times*, *USA Today* and *The Wall Street Journal*. Also, read the regional newspapers that cover your area, such as the *Los Angeles Times* for the West Coast or *The Boston Globe* in New England.

Magazines. Make it a point to read the major weekly newsmagazines, *Time* and *Newsweek*. Look at other magazines like *U.S. News and World Report*; it's aimed at older readers. Also, read the popular women's magazines. These magazines have a finely tuned understanding of the issues that attract women, the key adult demographic for your news. Also, newsstands are loaded with thousands of "niche" magazines on virtually every subject, and they are a constant source of story ideas. Don't

TIP THE LIBRARY

If you can't afford to buy these magazines, remember that your library will have most of the important ones. They also have important newspapers, such as the Sunday *New York Times*. Remember to look for the latest books in the news also.

forget to read your city or regional magazines.

Internet. One of the best places to spend time during the day is on the web, where you'll find most major newspapers, television networks and news wires. During the day you actually can watch stories and newscasts from other markets. For news junkies, the web is only going to become more and more important.

Radio. Don't forget to use the radio to keep informed. Radio is valuable for local breaking news and headlines. Most major markets have all-news or news-talk stations. National Public Radio's morning and afternoon news programs do a wonderful job on the big stories and on trend stories. Also, NPR is a good source for story ideas. Make it a habit to listen to the radio when you get up and on the drive to work, and then keep a radio near your desk in the newsroom.

How the World Works

It's not enough to be a news junkie and cultivate general knowledge. How can you properly write, report and edit the news if you don't know how the world works? You must understand the workings of such areas as medicine and health, business and economics, science and the environment, and education and the arts. Don't forget the criminal justice system, as well as politics and government. These subject areas are all major sources of news. They are complex; however, power producers know how they work.

News as a process. Most news involves developments, steps and stages. It's an ongoing process. You must learn the steps in the process. For example, local news covers the justice system from the time a crime is committed to when a suspect is arrested and then tried. Each story reports on a phase of the process.

The quiz. Power producers know all kinds of information related to these ongoing stories.

Do you know the difference between an arraignment and an indictment? What's the relationship between the NTSB and the FAA? How do doctors detect breast cancer? The Dow Jones measures what?

The answers. There are places to go to find answers. Try the research desk at the library or look on the web. Just about every institution in the universe has a web page, including federal, state and local governmental agencies. If you're looking for information, it's probably somewhere on the Internet. And if you really get desperate, just start working the telephones and asking questions.

The Producer as Reporter

In addition to knowing how the world works, power producers have basic reporting experience. They know how to collect the raw information of a news story and then assemble it into a story for a newscast. Power producers think and work like reporters.

Reporting skills. Why is it so important to have reporting skills? You need to use those skills to add depth and context to a story. At other times, you'll actually have to do original reporting. For instance, when you get a tip about a potential breaking story, you start working the telephones to add facts to the tip and verify the story. If the story is important, you'll have to get the details and then get a bulletin on the air.

Sources. Because power producers are also reporters, you need your own local news sources. Cultivating your own sources means you aren't dependent on anyone else in the newsroom for information. Start by building your own Rolodex with phone numbers of news contacts. This is excellent protection for when a big story breaks and the assignment desk is too busy to help. It's also priceless when you need to call in an interview guest at the last minute.

Time and dedication. Gaining general knowledge is a function of time as well as dedication. Decide now to take the time to learn, and dedicate yourself to continuing to gather information. Let it become a valuable obsession. But remember, as well informed as you might be at the moment, the news and what's important in the news is constantly evolving and changing. Who would have thought that power producers would need to know how White House interns are selected?

> **TIP**
> **REFERENCE BOOKS AND CD-ROMs**
>
>
> One way to double-check your facts is to keep a basic set of reference books on your desk. Include a current almanac, a Thesaurus, a dictionary, and telephone directories. Alice Main, editor of The Producer Newsletter, suggests "Grammar for Smart People" by Barry Tarshis, published in 1993 by Simon and Schuster. Also, obtain guides to local, state and federal government, including lists of office holders with addresses and telephone numbers. You can find maps, telephone cross-directories and encyclopedias on the Internet and on CD-ROMs.

CASE STUDY: CHICAGO PLANE CRASH

One evening while I was working as a producer at WBBM-TV in Chicago, we received a telephone tip that there was an airplane crash on the South Side, near Midway Airport. We had a vague location, so I grabbed the telephone cross-reference book. This book lists telephone numbers by street addresses instead of names. Then I started calling homes near the crash. I quickly learned that it was a United jet and that it had hit at least one home. This was enough information for a quick bulletin and to get our disaster plan in motion. The crash actually killed 45 passengers, including Michele Clark, who had been a reporter for our station and had just joined CBS News as a correspondent. If I had waited for an on-air reporter, the station would have been late in covering one of the major stories of the year.

In addition to being a journalist, a major part of being a successful producer is knowing your television market and its communities. The next chapter tells you why it's essential that you learn about these if you aspire to be a power producer.

Interview: Executive Producer

Alice Johnson Main
Executive Producer
WLS-TV
Chicago

Alice Johnson Main is executive producer at WLS-TV in Chicago. She is best known to producers as the editor and founder of The Producer Newsletter, a monthly e-mail newsletter, and a web site that includes the Producers' Book. A graduate of the University of Tulsa with a degree in communication, she has worked at WKRC-TV in Cincinnati, WDSU-TV in New Orleans, and KTUL-TV in Tulsa. As she puts it, "I've been an executive producer, producer and/or assignment editor in five newsrooms, in four cities, in 10 years." Since September 1997 she has been the supervising executive producer of the 11:30 a.m. and 5 p.m. newscasts at WLS, the ABC-owned station in Chicago.

What first attracted you to producing instead of the reporter/anchor track?

Hair. When you're a producer, your hair can look horrible and no one cares. In college we took turns in all of the roles: hosting, directing, camera, producing, etc. My hosting was decidedly so-so, and I do recall being more stressed about my hair than I was about preparing for my interviews. My directing was okay, but my technical directing was disastrous. I never could fully understand how to put a super on the air. My last turn was in the producer's chair. For some reason, I liked that.

I sensed power there. Soon after, I had my first internship. I knew I wanted to be a producer, so I asked for an internship in production. Brilliant, huh? I spent three days standing behind the studio camera operator, watching him zoom and pan, and trying to figure out how to get myself to the newsroom where I belonged. Someone at the station understood enough to let me switch, and then I was sure I wanted to be a producer. They were busy, barking out orders, and people really seemed to listen to them. In addition to my internship, I took a part-time job running the TelePrompTer, and then I was hooked. In between ripping scripts, I wrote stories for the producer. Those stories got me noticed when the next associate producer job opened up.

What do you know now that you would have liked to have known when you started as a producer?

I knew so little that I was a danger to the station and myself. I'm very lucky that I didn't do anything incredibly stupid or lawsuit-provoking. It was maybe five years ago that I recognized that it's really okay to admit what I don't know, and find a way to learn it.

What advice would you have for a producer just beginning his or her career?

Ask a lot of questions. Ask a lot of questions that begin with the word, "Why." "Why aren't we running this story on a bomb threat?" "Why can't we get a live shot out of Dubuque on this story?"

What do you enjoy most about producing?

That feeling you get maybe once every two weeks, when everything really comes together. The newscast sings and clicks, and you come out of the booth feeling like you're on top of the world.

What's the toughest challenge you faced as a producer?

Learning how to deal with people. I think I'm reasonably good at it now, but there was a time when I wasn't. One technique I use is what I call my "friendly phone-answering voice." I use this even when I'm incredibly busy. I don't just pick up the phone and bark out "NEWS!" But, "Newsroom, how may I help you?" Or even "Greetings, newsroom." The person on the other end of the line is already happy to be talking with me because he senses I'm a nice person. It starts the conversation off right. I also use that tone of voice when I talk over the public address system. If I need someone to call me right away, I page him or her using my absolute nicest voice. Not a hint of exasperation should creep in. And I try to include the word "Please."

How do you balance producing and your career with being a wife and mother?

Three words: Good child care. Three more words: An understanding husband. He's a newspaper reporter, and I've dragged him around the country a couple of times, but it's always worked out for him, too, eventually. As for the kids, one of them said to me recently, 'When are you and Dad going to get out of the news business?" When I asked him why, he said, 'Because you never get to take off work on holidays.'" He's terribly unimpressed by our jobs, and told his first-grade class that we were farmers.

As an executive producer, what do you look for when you're hiring producers?

I wish there were some magical way to answer that question. With hiring, it's a gut feeling as much as anything.

Chapter 3

Role One: Journalist

Where Do You Live?

In This Chapter:

- Understand Where You Live and Work
- What Is a Market?
- How Are the Market and Audience Linked?
- Producers Are Different from the Audience
- How To Learn About Your Market and Audience

Chapter 3: Where Do You Live?

> "Power producers realize that there's a critical difference between a television market and a real community."

It's a good news day. You have several potential lead stories. The Coast Guard has intercepted a freighter with 10 tons of marijuana on board, your chopper has footage of a high-speed chase, and the jury has been picked for an organized crime trial. Which is the best lead? It depends on where you live. Ten tons of marijuana would be a big deal in most markets, but not in Miami. A high-speed chase in Southern California is getting to be a routine event. The early stages of an organized crime trial might be big news in most markets, but not in Rhode Island.

A big factor in what's news depends on your station's market and audience. Because each market and community is different, your news judgment as a producer is going to be different. Because of this difference, power producers make a point of learning all they can about a market and community.

This chapter shows you exactly how to go about developing knowledge of your region. Also, power producers realize that there's a critical difference between a television market and a real community. You'll get some valuable tips about that, too.

Understand Where You Live and Work

Producing is transient. Young producers move around so much that they wind up in communities they don't know. Although producers advance their careers by moving to larger markets, too often they're strangers when they arrive and strangers when they leave. Needless to say, they never become power producers. This constant producer shuffle is only getting worse because there aren't enough qualified producers. More and more stations and cable operations are now doing newscasts. Small-market stations are adding newscasts in new time periods, and cable operators continue to add local and regional news channels.

Short-timers. Given these new opportunities, producers don't stay in their jobs long. According to an unpublished Freedom Forum study by Professor Vernon Stone at the University of Missouri's School of Journalism, the median stay at a station for producers is only about 2½ years. That's not a long time. Since that study was done, producer tenure may be even shorter, given the rapid increase in news programming. One result of this producer job shuffle is that producers assume every market is the same. They think the Phoenix audience is just like the Rochester audience.

Knowing little about the community, they produce newscasts aimed at the wrong audience. They become labeled as journeyman producers.

The solution. To avoid this career-killing label, get to know your new market quickly. Do so in an organized and disciplined fashion. Develop a plan and timetable for learning the market, and look at it as part of your job. Remember, this is an investment in your success at the station and in becoming a power producer. This isn't a casual exercise.

What Is a Market?

Before learning your market, you need to understand the difference between a television market and a community. The two terms are quite different.

Market. The word "market" is a television term. You hear it used in television newsrooms constantly. The term refers to a cluster of counties served by television stations usually licensed to a central city. This is the DMA, or Designated Market Area, defined by Nielsen Media Research. As a news producer, you take stories from a variety of different communities and try to make these stories useful and interesting to viewers in a DMA.

Community. Community means a town or city or a group of people sharing a common sense of place. In getting to understand your audience, this idea of community seems to be far easier to comprehend than something as artificial and arbitrary as a television market. Remember, you grew up in a community, not a television market.

Why market is important. In television news, you are forced to deal with this concept of a television market and a group of communities. Your station is selling advertising based on the market, so your success as a producer is based in part on your ability to generate ratings in the total market. One example of how a television market brings together diverse communities is Washington, the seventh-largest DMA. The market has 14 stations. The four major affiliates are located in the District, but there are stations in the Virginia and Maryland suburbs as well as one in West Virginia. There are two Spanish-language stations and at least two PBS stations. The Washington market also overlaps with the Baltimore DMA, and you can see those stations in Washington's Maryland suburbs. There is also a regional cable news channel. You might think Washington isn't a typical market because it's so large, but all television markets cover a broad region with a number of different communities. Think about the different "hyphenated" markets in which major stations are located in different cities that are miles apart, such as Florence-Myrtle Beach in South Carolina or Chico-Redding in California!

Don't forget the viewers. So for sales and marketing purposes, Nielsen defines your audience, the television market. Unfortunately, viewers don't think of themselves as living in some mythical television market. They could care less about something called a DMA. They don't even know they live in a DMA. The viewers actually think they live in a city, town, village or some other community with a zip code.

Community and news judgment. In making news judgments and weighing the value of stories, knowing a community is critical. As a producer you find yourself asking questions such as: "Does anyone outside that immediate town really care about this story?" Or, "Is this story so compelling that everyone in the market will be interested?" You run into these issues all the time. Knowing which stories are going to connect with the most viewers in the market is the mark of a power producer.

Dissimilar communities. By now you have the idea that television markets are spread out and diverse. Your station is broadcasting to all kinds of viewers. Like the Washington market, DMAs cover dissimilar communities: inner-city neighborhoods, suburbs and rural villages. These viewers certainly don't share common interests. They live very different lives. Let me give you an example of how complicated and difficult this can make life for you as a news producer. In Washington, producers have a difficult time making news decisions because of the diversity of the market. Audience research shows that viewers in Virginia, Maryland and the District don't care about news from the other parts of the market. In fact, audience research shows they aren't all that interested in news about the federal government, the largest employer, unless it involves their jobs and paychecks. The only ongoing story that seems to touch the entire market is any news about the Washington Redskins.

What's important? Producers in most markets face the same problems. No matter which market, in producing a newscast it's almost impossible to be all things to all people. This is a basic issue as you make all those judgments leading up to a rundown. However, your news decisions are easier if you understand your total market, its various communities and the audience.

TIP: LEARN DISTANCES

While driving around, try to figure out how long it takes to get to key locations from the station. This will help when you send a truck out to do a live shot. You'll know how long it might take the crew to get to a story.

How Are the Market and Audience Linked?

The nature of your station's market shapes virtually every type of story, whether crime, spot news, government, economy or environment. In deciding what to cover, how to cover it and how to present the news, your unique audience is the decisive factor.

Who are the viewers? The interest in certain stories varies dramatically based on the audience. For example, with lots of Irish descendants in the Northeast, "The Troubles" in Northern Ireland has local impact. The Boston stations regularly send reporters to cover Ireland, yet people in most parts of the country see the story as important but not of high local interest. In South Florida, there is interest in "The Troubles," but with a population that's half Hispanic (mostly Cuban), any major news involving Cuba or Latin America is local news. The point is that region and locale influence virtually every story. What's big news in one place is not big news somewhere else.

Every market is different. There is a saying in television news that every market is different. It's true, and you need to understand this and factor it into your newscast rundowns. Don't make a serious mistake and assume markets are the same. The result is normally a ratings embarrassment.

Producers Are Different from the Audience

Knowing your audience is a tough challenge. You're different in a number of ways from your typical viewer. Your life experience, interests and concerns differ from those of your audience. For one thing, the average person isn't going to invest in a college education to take a job that pays as little as a beginning producer's job!

Look around your newsroom. Look at your producing colleagues. They're young, college educated, mostly women and predominately white. If your own newsroom looks different, it's the exception.

The facts about producers. Based on Professor Vernon Stone's study, the median age for producers is 28. The University of Missouri professor says nine out of 10 producers are college-educated, and three-quarters majored in journalism or communications. His research also shows that the producer ranks are at least two-thirds female, with minorities underrepresented. Most minority producers are women. Based on my own observations, they're not married, don't have children and don't have a mortgage.

The facts about viewers. In contrast, your viewers are older, less well educated and make less money than producers. Those who watch your newscast are more likely to be from minority groups and male. Also, they are probably married, have children and a mortgage. Plus they seldom move out of the market. The audience is also more conservative than young producers. A consulting firm, Audience Research & Development, has run focus groups contrasting the newscast interests of viewers and newspeople. What the viewers find valuable is often quite different from what people in the newsroom find valuable.

How To Learn About Your Market and Audience

How do you go about understanding a market? How do you get to know your audience personally? How do you, as a transient, college-educated producer, learn about the place and audience where you live and work? This is difficult but critically important if you want to be successful.

Get started right away. If you don't, you'll begin to absorb your newsroom colleagues' assumptions about the market. They're often wrong. If you learn about the market in a quick but systematic way, then you'll be able to test those assumptions based on personal experience. There's another reason you need to be a quick study: You are already making news decisions every day in your newscast, and you can't afford to make a bad call.

Here are more ideas for learning the market:

Read the newspapers. Even before you arrive in a market, even before your first job interview, read the local newspapers. Read them first from their web pages. If you can't, buy a paper as soon as you arrive in town. Don't limit your reading to the big daily newspaper. Remember that there may be more than one daily in the market. Read the small weekly community newspapers as well. And don't overlook the local business weekly. One of the favorite issues of local business papers is an annual top 25 list of things like employers, hospitals, broadcast stations, cities and supermarkets. It provides great background. If you're a news junkie you also probably love newsstands. Find a good one that has all the local newspapers.

Buy books about the area. Big bookstores, such as Borders or Barnes & Noble, have sections for regional books. See if you can find a good history of your new city or region. They also may have books on other topics you need to know about, such as guides to state government and histories of local companies.

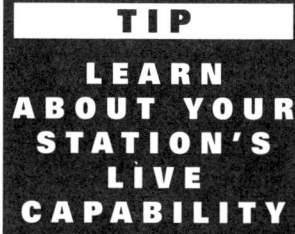

TIP
LEARN ABOUT YOUR STATION'S LIVE CAPABILITY

In the first week, before things are too crazy, go out on a live shot. See how well your station's trucks work and how long it takes to get a report on the air. It will be incredibly helpful to know the time it takes a crew to get to a location and to set up. It saves you from sending out a crew without enough time to make air. Not allowing enough time for set-up is a major complaint from photographers.

PRODUCERS SHARE SOME ADVICE

How do other producers learn about their communities? At one workshop I asked this question and received great suggestions. Here's their list, slightly edited:

- Buy a map book and learn it
- Make your own Rolodex from scratch
- Take public transportation, ride around
- Read *all* the local papers
- Visit local cafes and hangouts and listen to the conversations
- Go into the field with the crews, especially with the best local photographer
- Join clubs and organizations
- Tour the city
- Volunteer at a church or a synagogue or a community group
- Listen to local talk radio
- Go to city council or town meetings
- Have the station assign a buddy familiar with the area
- Identify community leaders and set up a meeting
- Get information packets from the Chamber of Commerce and visitors bureau
- Hold a brown bag newsroom lunch with newsmakers
- Go to a library or a bookstore for regional history and tour guides
- Talk to your hairdresser or barber
- And my favorite: "Get lost."

The ideas on this list are invaluable: Take them and organize your own campaign. Your campaign will parallel your development as a news junkie, but with an entirely different purpose.

Invest in a good map. These same bookstores, or newsstands, will have map books of the region. Get a good one—a big one—and memorize it. Better yet, buy two: one for your car and one for your desk.

Surf the Internet. Most chambers of commerce and tourist or visitor's bureaus have web pages. Take a tour using your computer. You'll be amazed at what you can find about your new market. There will also be restaurant and shopping guides, maps and local government sites. Go to your favorite Internet search engine and type in your area. This research should keep you off the streets and out of trouble for days.

Ask the business community for help. The chamber and economic development people create packets of information for businesses looking to relocate to the region. These packets are valuable for you as a producer because they include population data, information on the local economy and local education resources.

Drive around. Now take your map book and organize a drive through all the city neighborhoods. Visit newsworthy landmarks and smaller towns. Make a grid and spend your days off driving through the region until you've really seen the market. Don't miss any part of it. When you drive around, don't forget to stop and get out of the car. Talk to people, and visit the important landmarks. Develop a sense of each community.

Hitch a ride with your photographers. You also want to ride with the photographers, particularly those with the best local knowledge. Go with them to locations where your newsroom regularly does live shots, such as the airport, city hall, convention center, courthouses and big malls. Find out the logistics problems they face at these locations.

Get involved. Producers tend to be younger, with no children, and they work odd shifts. They tend to socialize with other people from broadcasting. This makes it difficult to get to know people in the market and community. One piece of advice for producers is to develop a social life away from the newsroom. Get a real life, away from fellow broadcasters.

Offer to help out. Volunteering is another great way to learn about the market. It also helps you meet people and gives you more of an emotional stake in the community. Be careful, however, about potential conflicts of interest.

All of these ideas are excellent ways for you to get involved and to learn your market. Even if you've been at a station for some time, it's not too late to start. If you still don't know where all the towns in your market are, get going! Once you begin to understand your market, let that information help you report the news the audience wants and needs, the most important part of being a journalist.

Chapter 4

Role One: Journalist

Getting the News

In This Chapter:

- Break Out of the Box
- Grow Your Own Stories
- How To Find News
- Traditional News Sources
- Own the Big Stories

Chapter 4: Getting the News

"As a producer, it's your newscast. If a bad newscast runs, don't try to duck responsibility."

The early-show producer is whining. It's almost four o'clock and he doesn't have a good lead story. He's blaming a brain-dead assignment desk, lazy reporters and the heartless news gods, who are all out to destroy his newscast. It's everyone's fault but his. Perhaps he should stop trying to spread the blame and look at himself.

As a producer, it's your newscast. If a bad newscast runs, don't try to duck responsibility. It's up to you to actively work on news coverage. If you don't, then you're no better than the "stackers and packers." When it comes to getting the right stories for your newscast, you must be proactive.

Power producers make sure they have strong stories. They generate a mix of stories to create successful, balanced newscasts. They go beyond the news found on the wires, and they get away from the routine. Power producers develop a "vision" for creative news coverage.

In this chapter, you'll examine problems associated with traditional daily news sources and see how you can serve your viewers better by encouraging enterprise reporting. You'll learn how to win the big stories that are critical to the station's long-term success and your own.

Break Out of the Box

If you looked at thousands of newscasts, you'd probably agree that most are dull and routine. The stories aren't interesting, and most of the news isn't important. That's a sad commentary on producing.

Why are so many newscasts boring? You can point at unmotivated reporters, overworked assignment editors and weak leadership from news directors, but don't ignore uninspired producers.

You can break out of dull and routine coverage. Even better, prevent it from happening. The place to start is with the raw material, the news itself. Much of it is predictable and not terribly valuable. For example, stories about traffic accidents, supermarket openings and the governor's visit to your town may look like news but mean little to your viewers and their lives.

Instead of accepting this daily list of trivial events, power producers sift through the raw material to find valuable stories. Or they work to develop stories that actually belong in the newscast. They measure the value of stories against a coverage concept that matches their newscast vision.

For your newscast, a vision means a news identity. To create a vision for your program, determine what types of stories are important and interesting to your audience. A consistent vision encourages your audience to rely on your station because they find value in its newscasts. An example of a station that understands its news vision is Philadelphia's WPVI-TV.

In the early 1970s, WPVI developed "Action News" as a news identity. The format consists of brief stories, short reporter packages and active-voice writing. Over the years, the newsroom has created a strong sense of just what kinds of stories fit its news identity. This consistent vision has helped WPVI dominate the local news ratings in the fourth largest market for three decades. Although critics say "Action News" covers too much spot news and crime, WPVI has a successful news identity.

Delivering such a vision is a two-step process. First, help the newsroom understand what kind of news you need for your newscast. Second, get the news covered properly. This is difficult because news coverage is a collaborative process.

It takes a team to cover the news and deliver a newscast vision. If your newscast doesn't have a clearly defined news identity, the assignment editors will cover what they think is important, and they may not fully understand the news needs of your audience. Prevent misunderstandings by articulating a consistent newscast vision to everyone in the newsroom, including assignment editors, reporters and photographers. They all must clearly understand and support your vision.

Grow Your Own Stories

Whatever vision you create, you need stories that draw viewers and encourage them to stay tuned. The answer to dull and routine newscasts is "enterprise reporting." That term describes original reporting, or the effort of developing a story exclusive to your newsroom. In television news, enterprise reporting is more often the exception than the rule. A power producer encourages enterprise reporting and sets expectations.

Power producers foster enterprise reporting through advance preparation. Here are some suggestions:
- Set a personal goal of coming to work with at least two original story ideas each day.
- Work ahead. Talk to reporters about story ideas for the next day.
- Be prepared to brief a reporter on the details of your story ideas, including possible interviews.
- Encourage story proposals from everyone in the newsroom, not just reporters and producers. Photographers frequently know the most about the community.
- Review the coverage planners put out by the Associated Press.

By anticipating events, you'll have time to work on creative coverage. It's all front-end work. You might argue that you don't have time to spend on enterprise reporting. Can you afford not to spend the time? Isn't this as important as supervising pre-production?

If you want to encourage reporters to do enterprise reporting, then make it important. Here's how to communicate that urgency:
- Find a way to reward the reporter who comes up with the best or most original stories.
- Openly praise and celebrate enterprise reporting in the newsroom.
- Hold reporters accountable for regularly making beat calls on topics like education, medicine and business, which fall outside the realm of spot news.

How To Find News

Power producers look at their entire world for potential stories. They don't limit themselves to the wires, newspapers and the competition. Relevant and interesting news stories are all around. For instance:
- You see something on the way to work, like a big increase in gas prices.
- Your neighbor tells you about a local zoning scandal.
- A flyer from an organization you belong to warns about a new environmental threat.
- A relative who works for a governmental agency tells you about a potential lawsuit.
- Complaint calls or letters to the newsroom prompt a follow-up story on a sensitive topic.
- A friend develops a disease you've never heard about.

When you're involved in your community, you'll hear things before you see news releases. But don't be the only news hound at your station. Encourage everyone to be alert for potential enterprise stories and to contribute story ideas. People in your newsroom live in different parts of the market and have a wide variety of relationships and news contacts. They know what's happening in their communities. This is one reason why newsrooms and stations should have diverse staffs. They offer more opportunity for broader coverage.

Traditional News Sources

Of course, you can't ignore the traditional news sources. Much of your basic daily news coverage comes from those sources. However, power producers only use traditional news sources as a base. They supplement them with enterprise reporting and general knowledge to add perspective and context to the news. Here's how to make the best use of traditional news sources.

The wires. It's easy to become dependent on the wire services, mainly the AP. Right there in front of you on a computer screen is a complete story. It's a trap, however. Don't think the wire services are the best or final version of a story. Power producers check out wire stories and then filter

TIP
TEST FOR ENTERPRISE

Remember, test every enterprise story idea against your newscast vision. Does it fit the news identity?

> **TIP**
> ## ADVANCE THE STORY
>
>  When you have no choice but to follow up a story from the morning paper—or any other outside source—always advance the story. Never let a reporter do the same story the newspaper published. This is unprofessional and a disservice to your viewers. They don't deserve warmed-over news. Find a new angle, one the newspaper story missed, or take the story to the next development.

each story through their news vision. The wire services are a tool, so treat them like a tip service. Make calls, verify information and question the original sources to see if there is more to the story. Be a reporter.

I learned this lesson the day an anchor turned to me and wanted to know which statistics he should use in a copy story. The AP and UPI had posted different numbers for fatalities in a traffic accident. The anchor looked to me for an answer. I suggested he call the sheriff's office or state troopers where the accident happened. That was a startling new idea for him. And as you might expect, he then thought I ought to make the call.

One problem with using wire stories is the way they are reported. They don't always contain the best local hook to sell the story to the audience. Also, because the AP is owned by newspapers, it tends to string information together newspaper-style, using an inverted pyramid story structure. Power producers must rewrite wire copy in a conversational style and do reporting to find the key elements that sell the story.

Despite their drawbacks, wire services can help you stay current on news leads. Develop a pattern of checking the wires every few minutes for breaking stories or new developments. And be sure to check the wires before going on air and even during the newscast.

Newspapers. A power producer uses local and national newspapers as a tip sheet for story ideas. With their larger staffs, newspapers can cover a topic in more depth than television stations can. Local papers always cover lots of regional stories. *However, never use newspapers as the final source for a story.* Advance the story with reporting. Don't be lazy.

Smaller local newspapers are a great source for story ideas. Weeklies are a place to find those quirky little stories that add a "moment" to your newscast. But don't just subscribe to these papers and shove them under your stack of reading material. Assign a responsible person to read and clip them.

National newspapers like *The New York Times*, *USA Today* and *The Wall Street Journal* offer story ideas you might not find elsewhere. When CBS News correspondent Eric Engberg taught journalism at the University of Missouri, he told students that anyone can find at least two potential local stories in *The New York Times* every day. He's right. Most government reports first appear in the *Times*. Read these reports and see if they apply to your community. For example, a study on teenage smoking or a report on hot new jobs can be developed into local stories.

Radio. Radio news is not what it used to be, but there are still good stations doing excellent local news. If your market has an all-news station or a strong local news station, listen to it daily. Radio news is superb at reporting local breaking stories.

The competition. Another source for news stories is other stations' newscasts. Every once in a while, the competition beats you on a story. Be alert. Smart producers have someone—usually a desk assistant or an intern—log the competition while your newscast is on the air. Have the person call you if they think you've missed something important. However, never trust facts from the competition. Confirm and advance the story using your own sources.

Beat calls. Power producers start with the discipline of regular beat calls and are vigilant about staying on top of spot news coverage. On an hourly basis, using a standard list of telephone numbers, have a production assistant or intern call every law-enforcement agency and fire department in the region as a potential source for breaking news.

Bear in mind that beat calls are frustrating. Interns or production assistants get tired of hourly calls, particularly when nothing's going on. Regardless, make them responsible for building a consistent routine. Emphasize the importance of developing a positive,

>
> **TIP**
> ## USE THE RADIO
>
>  Set up a radio in your newsroom with a timer so you automatically hear the local hourly newscasts. It pays off when they report the breaking story your desk missed!

POWER PRODUCER: A PRACTICAL GUIDE TO TV NEWS PRODUCING

friendly relationship with the agencies. If they do, you stand a good chance of getting a call when something breaks, or at least a tip during the beat call.

Scanners. Scanner reports are another major source of spot stories. Your newsroom should have a bank of scanner radios tuned to the various local law-enforcement agencies. A police or fire call on the scanners is your first indication of a major breaking news event.

Normally, scanners are located near the assignment desk. If you can't hear them from your work area, you might want your own set of scanners nearby. They can be loud, intrusive and annoying, but you rely on them. Don't allow others to turn down the volume. Also, learn the local codes. Learn to identify the way voices change when important calls come in. Stations in larger markets sometimes employ people to monitor the scanners.

Never report something you heard on the scanner or in a tip without verifying the story. Call the agency involved and confirm the story. Get as much information as possible before going on the air. Although this is common sense, producers and reporters have failed to confirm stories properly. They end up embarrassing their stations and themselves.

Tip calls. Stations receive these in several ways. Some stations promote a news-tip hotline linked to a special cellular telephone number. Tips on these lines save precious minutes in covering a breaking story, and let viewers know the station values their input.

News releases. Every day the assignment desk receives reams of news releases from all sorts of organizations, from government agencies to small businesses. Remember, sometimes you actually get news from news releases. Just don't take a story directly from a news release.

News conferences. News conferences are called so people can present their views to many media representatives at one time. News conferences and video news releases (VNRs) are often self-serving. This is not a good way to cover the news. You get only one side of the story, and you need to tell both sides. News conferences also make boring television. If the story is worth doing, then report on the people directly involved.

VNRs. These are worse than news conferences because a reporter can't ask questions. The organization that paid for the VNR wants your station to run its version of a story intact. This is hardly reporting, and it often isn't news. Some VNRs are blatant ads for products. Be on guard.

If you have to run a VNR or file tape supplied by an outside source, disclose the source of the video. Identify who paid for the video and sent it to the station. Use a super and a line in your copy. Such acknowledgment used to be station policy, but it seems to have lapsed in recent years. You must be honest with your audience.

Reporter beats. The best way to get original stories is through a beat system. Newspapers assign reporters to regularly cover local institutions like city hall, schools and businesses. Beats give newspapers an edge because they start with reporters who focus on specific topics and cultivate key sources.

Unfortunately, few television newsroom managers can afford to assign reporters to regular beats. There just aren't enough reporters. However, there are ways to get around budget and staffing limitations. One solution is to assign areas of expertise. Find out which subjects your reporters like to cover. Then give them those areas as informal beats and ask them to stay current on the topics.

Own the Big Stories

Capturing a big story is every power producer's dream. Such stories include a major airplane crash, a weather disaster like a hurricane or tornado, or a dramatic rescue attempt. These stories are so important and have such a wide impact that they draw viewers to the station with the best coverage. Cable and broadcast stations know this, and are recognized for doing outstanding work on major stories. Channels that sweep the news ratings make their reputation by "owning" the big stories. Here are some techniques to help you do that.

Roll everything. To own a major story, don't hesitate or hold back resources. When really big stories break, the audience starts to hunt for the best coverage and latest information. That's why it's critical to get your station on the story immediately. When a story is of vital interest to your audience, pull out all the stops. Don't let limited resources get in your way. Be creative. If you need a satellite truck but your station doesn't own one, see if you can rent one, use another station's truck, or beg time from your network if they're on scene.

Team coverage. One way to own a big story is through team coverage. This means assigning reporters to cover every aspect of the story. Using team coverage demonstrates a commitment to doing a thorough job on a story viewers care about. Highlight that commitment with team-coverage graphics and copy lines. Team coverage is partly a promotional device, but it's also good journalism for important stories.

Stay with the story. Big stories can tax newsroom attention spans. When everyone in the newsroom is tired of the story, the audience frequently wants more. So stay with the story for its duration. Find new and different angles. Again, this is another good reason to get to know your community and audience.

Covering disasters. Every newsroom needs a disaster plan. Does your newsroom have one? This gets your newsroom moving quickly on a major story with minimum confusion. A disaster plan can't possibly cover every contingency or every potential disaster, but the best plans are flexible and updated often. No two stories are going to unfold the same, but all contain some of the same elements. For example, local hospitals need to be covered if a disaster causes injuries, and you'll need coverage from the shelters if an evacuation occurs.

The disaster plan should list assignments. For example, it should assign producers to handle bulletins; to staff the control room for continuous coverage; to act as liaison between the desk, tape editing and the show producers; and to handle requests from other stations and the networks.

A key part of any disaster coverage includes assigning key reporters and anchors to the areas they know best. Put your best reporters and key

---

WARNING! ETHICS CHALLENGE

In covering virtually any major story, you and your newsroom will be faced with ethical issues. The Radio-Television News Directors Association has guidelines for covering large-scale, breaking events. Written by The Poynter Institute's Bob Steele, and widely distributed after shootings at Columbine High School in Littleton, CO, the following guidelines should be included in your newsroom's disaster plan and posted in the newsroom.

Guidelines for Covering Hostage-Taking Crises, Police Raids, Prison Uprisings or Terrorist Action

In covering an ongoing crisis situation, journalists are advised to:

■ Always assume the hostage-taker, gunman or terrorist has access to the reporting.

■ Avoid describing with words or showing with still photography or video any information that could divulge the tactics or positions of SWAT team members.

■ Fight the urge to become a player in any standoff, hostage situation or terrorist incident. Journalists should become personally involved only as a last resort and with the explicit approval of top news management and the consultation of trained hostage negotiators on the scene.

■ Be forthright with viewers, listeners or readers about why certain information is being withheld if security reasons are involved.

■ Seriously weigh the benefits of disseminating information to the public against the potential harm that information might cause. This is especially important in live reporting of an ongoing situation.

■ Strongly resist the temptation to telephone a gunman or hostage-taker. Journalists generally aren't trained in negotiation techniques, and one wrong question or inappropriate word could jeopardize someone's life. Furthermore, just calling in could tie up phone lines or otherwise complicate negotiators' communication efforts.

■ Notify authorities immediately if a hostage-taker or terrorist calls the newsroom. Also, have a plan ready for how to respond.

■ Challenge any gut reaction to "go live" from the scene of a hostage-taking crisis, unless there are strong journalistic reasons for a live, on-the-scene report. Things can go wrong very quickly in a live report, which may endanger lives or damage

TIP: DEVELOP A CHECKLIST

 When a big story breaks, it's difficult to remember everything that needs to be done. Through experience, power producers develop a mental checklist of what to do during crisis time or as a major story unfolds. They know that they can't miss a potential angle. Here's a checklist to help you pull together coverage of a big story.

- **Graphics.** Use banners and graphic headlines as well as special anchor boxes to remind the audience of the depth of your coverage. Don't forget charts, graphs and full-screen information to explain the story. Ask yourself whether a timeline graphic would be possible or helpful.
- **Experts.** Quickly locate the most knowledgeable experts and make them a part of your news team for that story. This is another reason why you need to build a list of sources and contacts and get to know your community.
- **Community involvement.** If it's appropriate to the story, find a way to involve the community. For example, you might spearhead a food or fund drive for hurricane victims, or report on one that's already taking place.
- **Maps.** Show viewers exactly where the story happened in relation to their community.
- **Phoners.** If you can't get a live report, then use telephone reports from reporters in the field. Have graphics prepared ahead of time with a photograph of each reporter that can be displayed with a map or other graphic from the story.
- **Sidebars.** What's happening of interest or importance around the main story? Add perspective and context to a big story by looking for the human element. If possible, report on the people directly affected by a major event.
- **History.** How did the story develop? Has this happened before? Who are the key players? Dig up details to add more perspective and context.
- **Instant special.** News management should consider doing an instant special as soon as possible.

---

negotiations. Furthermore, ask if the value of a live report is really justified compared with the harm that could occur.

- Give no information, factual or speculative, about a hostage-taker's mental condition, state of mind or reasons for actions while a standoff is in progress. The value of such information to the audience is limited, and the possibility of such characterizations exacerbating an already dangerous situation are quite real.
- Give no analyses or comments on a hostage taker's or terrorist's demands. As bizarre, ridiculous or even legitimate as such demands may be, it's important that negotiators take all demands seriously.
- Keep news helicopters out of the standoff area because their noise can create communication problems for negotiators and their presence could prompt a gunman to take deadly action.
- Do not report information obtained from police scanners. If law-enforcement personnel and negotiators are compromised in their communications, their attempts to resolve a crisis are greatly complicated.
- Be very cautious about reporting on the medical condition of hostages until after a crisis concludes. Also, be cautious when interviewing hostages or released hostages while a crisis continues.
- Exercise care when interviewing family members or friends of those involved in standoff situations. Make sure the interview legitimately advances the story for the public and is not simply conducted for the shock value of the emotions conveyed or as a conduit for the interviewee to transmit messages to specific individuals.
- Go beyond the basic story of the hostage-taking or standoff to report on the larger issues behind the story. Examine the how and why of what happened, the preparation and execution of the SWAT team, or other issues related to the incident.

In covering a pending raid or law-enforcement action, journalists are advised to:

- Be extremely careful not to compromise the secrecy of officials' planning and execution. Reporters and photographers accompanying officers or staking out raid locations should very cautious about how they act, where they go and what clues they may inadvertently reveal that might compromise the raid's execution. Journalists should check and double-check planning efforts.

Bob Steele,
The Poynter Institute

anchors in the field. If the disaster is big enough, have them anchor from the scene. This is an opportunity to show off their reporting skills.

Winning every day. Doing the best job on the big running stories and major events or disasters is important. But remember, a station also wins through consistency, by outdoing the competition on every newscast. You win in the ratings by having a solid, well-executed vision every day.

Your first role, that of broadcast journalist, offers unique challenges and rewards. In the next chapter, you'll learn about another role of a power producer, that of news writer. Every power producer must be an excellent broadcast news writer. In the next chapter, you'll learn how to write copy that informs and holds the viewers.

Chapter 5

**Role Two:
News Writer**

Writing Broadcast News

In This Chapter:

- The Five C's of Broadcast News
- Dumb Words
- Leads That Sell
- Story Structure
- Basic Rules
- Writing to Video
- Writing Tips

Chapter 5: Writing Broadcast News

> "Use everyday words, but make them accurate and precise, powerful and informal."

Dan Rather looked into the camera with that Texas sincerity and intoned, "From Washington this evening comes word ..."

Yes, the highly paid anchor of the CBS Evening News used one of the worst clichés of "journalese," the stilted writing found in newspapers and on the wires. As a news producer, you're constantly bombarded by journalese. It's no wonder that it creeps into your copy.

You must avoid this writing disease if you want to be a power producer! Mastery of conversational newswriting is absolutely essential. In this chapter you will learn about conversational writing and how to write clear, understandable stories. You'll find out how to write leads that sell, and how to avoid the dumb words that deaden broadcast copy. The chapter closes with specific tips to make your copy shine.

The Five C's of Broadcast News Writing

Understandably, much of the writing you did in school wasn't consistent with broadcast news writing. Your compositions for English class are meant to be read, but not aloud. Writing for the ear is different from writing for the eye. You are writing copy so an anchor or reporter can tell the viewers the story. To write copy for the ear you must learn and practice the five C's: Conversational, Clear, Concise, Compelling, Cliché Free.

Conversational. When writing broadcast copy, you write for the ear. Because the audience both hears and sees the news, television is the most powerful means of informing the public yet devised. But there is a drawback: Your viewers get only one chance to grasp the story. This means you must use conversational language because it's what people are used to hearing. It helps them understand a story quickly.

Write the way people talk. Think about how you respond when someone asks you about what happened in your day. You don't answer them by talking about routine events—you tell them immediately about the most important and exciting thing that happened. So give the viewer the most important part of the story first. Also, in conversation you seldom use complex sentences with parenthetical phrases or restrictive clauses. Don't do it in broadcast news writing either. Phrases and clauses should be separate sentences.

Broadcast news copy may strive to be simple, but write with respect for your listener. You'll hear consultants and news directors talk about your average viewer as "Joe Six-pack." That's to help you understand that the audience is different from the newsroom staff, but it doesn't mean that Joe and family aren't smart. Treat them with respect.

Don't let the idea of conversational writing fool you. It's not slick or casual. You don't use slang or jargon. Conversational writing is grammatically correct. It is disciplined writing. Use everyday words, but make them accurate and precise, powerful and informal.

Clear. Limit sentences to one idea. This makes it easier for the listener to comprehend an idea. Any time you start to use a conjunction like "and" or a comma, look at the sentence. It may be getting too complicated.

Always put the attribution first. In broadcast writing put the attribution before a statement to clarify the source of a statement. A quote before attribution sounds like the anchor's opinion. It's confusing. Example:

BAD: "This is the biggest case of embezzlement I've ever seen," said the mayor.

BETTER: The mayor said this is the biggest case of embezzlement he's ever seen.

TIP
READ, READ, READ

Even if you have a degree from one of the best journalism schools, reading books on broadcast newswriting is time well spent. There is a list of excellent books in the Resources for Producers section at the end of the book.

Avoid names in the lead sentence. Broadcast writers sometimes put a name in the lead sentence. This practice gets in the way of clear understanding. For instance, "Forty-four-year-old Fred Furd was accidentally ejected from his home today." Now the story gets interesting. "Police say the prominent local newscaster was ejected after his television exploded." At this point, because the story sounds interesting, if not strange, the listener is actually paying attention but can't remember the name of the victim. Avoid using a name in the first sentence if possible. If you can't, be sure to repeat the name later in your copy.

Don't use too many numbers. Numbers are difficult to follow when listening to the news. Make them easy to understand. Limit yourself to one number per sentence, and never put a number first in a sentence—it's confusing.

BAD: Thirteen people died when the train went off the tracks near St. Louis, but some 150 passengers survived the tenth railroad accident this year.

BETTER: A rail accident near St. Louis killed 13 passengers. At least 150 passengers escaped the latest accident on the railroad. This is the railroad's 10th accident this year.

Avoid officialese. Officialese is the special jargon of an organization or profession. It's designed to impress, intimidate, and otherwise keep the average person out of the club. Your listeners find it tough to understand. Police are the worst offenders, followed closely by physicians and bureaucrats.

BAD: Forty-four-year-old Deborah Staff was shot by another officer in an effort to terminate her use of deadly force.

BETTER: Police say they shot the woman when she threatened an officer.

Be alert, because everybody uses jargon. Jargon slips into the language in words like interface and bottom line. If you aren't careful, it's easy to interview people and then repeat their words to the audience. For example, a New York State Thruway accident killed two members of a family. Reporters for all three local stations in live reports said the driver was "ejected" from the vehicle, and then ran a taped interview from a state trooper who said the victim was ejected from the vehicle. The conversational word is "thrown," a more powerful verb.

Avoid 50-cent words. It's not clear writing if the listener is wondering what a fancy word means. You aren't here to impress viewers but to inform them. Use plain words to communicate fancy ideas. Don't look for a synonym just because you've used a word before in your copy. Keep your words simple and clear.

Concise. Use simple declarative sentences. The declarative sentence is the heart of effective broadcast news writing. Put your subject first, followed by the verb, and then the object. This is the SVO structure. Such sentences are stronger and easier to understand.

Write short sentences. Research has found that short sentences are easier to understand and more powerful than longer ones. There's no mandatory sentence length, but try to keep your sentences to fewer than 20 words. Since you are writing for the ear, mix your sentence length to avoid a singsong delivery.

Compelling. Write in the active voice. Broadcast news writers use active voice for more powerful and interesting writing. Active voice is also more precise, and creates shorter SVO sentences. Writing active voice is hard to do well or consistently, but it's the mark of a power producer. A classic example:

BAD: The ball was hit by John to the outfielder.

BETTER: John hit the ball to the outfielder.

Use the present tense. News is happening now. If the event you are writing about is still underway, then say so. Don't make a story past tense when it's not necessary.

BAD: Police issued an all points bulletin for a suspect in the robbery.

BETTER: Police have an all points bulletin out for a robbery suspect.

Sometimes it seems that you have no choice, because the event is over, but there are other ways to keep a story current.

BAD: Police have arrested a suspect in that robbery.

BETTER: Police are now questioning a suspect in that robbery.

When you can't avoid it, don't force the issue. Phony present tense sounds awkward and confusing.

Emphasize the time element in your copy. Television news is immediate. Refer to a time of day, such as "Police late this afternoon ..." This gives the story immediacy. Avoid the word "today" because it's used so much that it's meaningless and slows down your copy. Instead, refer to the time of day, such as evening or late morning. Also, never start a story with the word yesterday, because it's no longer news.

Cliché free. Clichés are a drug on television news. They poison your stories. While these overused words are often imprecise, even misleading, trying to keep clichés out of your writing is tough. Even a power producer has a hard time living Cliché free. Still, your goal is a cliché-free newscast.

Newspapers have developed a special language of clichés they use in headlines and copy. Words like probe and heist are two words found in newspapers because they save space. These words aren't conversational.

Adjectives and adverbs contribute to the cliché problem. Don't use adjectives and avoid adverbs. For instance, "In war-ravaged Sarajevo, a truce tonight ..." or "Strife-torn Belfast is peaceful after a day of riots." Better yet, don't tell your viewers Sarajevo is heavily damaged—show them damaged buildings and rubble on tape.

Dumb Words

Beyond clichés is another category of words that you might call "dumb words." These are useless words that producers, writers and reporters rely on too frequently. Most of these words actually indicate that you don't have the correct information or proper attribution. Many fit in the category of phony attribution.

Allegedly. This is the most useless cliché in broadcast copy. Many broadcast news writers

CLICHÉS ON PARADE

Here is a list of clichés collected by former CBS and CNN correspondent Deborah Potter. Potter is now executive director of the News Lab training program in Washington.

- at the end of the day
- battle lines are drawn
- beast of burden
- brutal slaying
- burn the midnight oil
- campaign trail
- chalk up a victory
- chickens coming home to roost
- closer to home
- cream of the crop
- crystal clear
- delegate-rich California
- dream team
- an eye for an eye
- easy prey
- even as we speak
- fall on deaf ears
- far cry
- few and far between
- foot in the door
- from time immemorial
- give a green light
- goes without saying
- golfball-sized hail
- gone but not forgotten
- grief-stricken widow
- grim consequences
- gunned down
- hail of bullets
- hale and hearty
- hat in the ring
- hit the nail on the head
- horse of a different color
- hot and heavy
- in no uncertain terms
- innocent bystander
- innocent victim
- in the final analysis
- it remains to be seen
- last but not least
- last nail in the coffin
- leave in a huff
- loom on the horizon
- long holiday weekend
- loud and clear
- marked contrast
- mute evidence
- mother nature
- near death's door
- needless to say
- nip in the bud
- no holds barred
- nose to the grindstone
- oil-rich Middle East
- only time will tell
- parents' worst nightmare
- powers that be
- proud as a peacock
- ringing off the hook
- selling like hotcakes
- send a clear signal
- sigh of relief
- skating on thin ice
- smelling like a rose
- strategic waterway
- sword of Damocles
- tension is high
- tempers flared
- thick and fast
- tie the knot
- tough as nails
- trigger happy
- under his belt
- uneasy truce
- ups and downs
- veritable smorgasbord
- violence flared
- vital stake
- water over the dam
- water under the bridge
- the white stuff
- whopping increase
- widespread fear
- wrong place at the wrong time

throw in the word "allegedly" because they don't want to inadvertently report that someone is guilty of a crime. For some reason, producers, reporters and even news directors think this word provides some kind of legal shield. It doesn't. What they should do is provide proper attribution. You need proper sources for your information about someone accused of a crime, sources like the police or the district attorney's office. You need someone to make an allegation.

Reportedly. This is another word favored by producers and reporters too lazy to get accurate information or clear attribution. "Reportedly, the victim was killed on impact." Exactly how were they killed? Who says? If you don't know that something is a fact, then don't say it might be true. The use of "reportedly" makes a statement tentative.

Apparently. This is a close relative of reportedly. "Apparently the accident victim is dead." Is this a fact or not? Apparently you aren't a very good reporter because you don't know.

Undetermined. "The police say they have a suspect in custody but the motive for the crime is undetermined." If you don't know, don't try to hide the fact. This is another non-conversational word from the journalese dictionary. Have you ever heard someone use "undetermined" in a real conversation?

Suspect. This word is often misused; it means police have a specific person in mind as the person who committed a crime. You have heard the popular line, "The suspect fled on foot." Sloppy reporters use "suspect" when referring to someone who should be labeled by criminal type, such as robber or burglar. Unless there's a clear identity and that person is known, don't use "suspect."

Officials say. "Officials say" can be called phony attribution. Closely related are "some say" and "experts report." Either you know who said something or you don't. If you don't know the source, don't make up a vague source.

Recent reports. You hear stories refer to "recent reports" constantly. For example: "Researchers recently reported that broadcast newswriting isn't understandable." What reports? When? This is lazy and imprecise reporting. Sometimes producers and reporters use this phrase because the story isn't timely and they are trying to hide that fact. When the report was delivered and who wrote the report may be important. Be specific.

This list could go on and on. Virtually everyone writing broadcast copy under deadline slips into using these dumb words. However, power producers keep clichés, journalese, and phony or imprecise attribution out of their copy and newscast.

Leads That Sell

Each story in your newscast must start with a strong lead sentence. The most effective lead refers to some aspect of the story important or interesting to the audience—the "hook." Identify something in the story that will hook the viewers and use it in the lead sentence. Such leads keep viewers watching.

Put a "hook" in the lead. Here's an example of a weak but common lead: "The Smallville City Council voted to increase property tax rates by 10 cents last night." (And then the story goes on to other things like the amount of additional revenue the tax will generate.) Here's a better solution: "If you live in Smallville, you're going to pay more property tax next year. The city council is raising your taxes an average of 600 dollars." The best lead lines involve the audience by relating the news to them. Find a viewer benefit and get the viewers involved in the story.

TIP — WHERE'S THE HOOK? If you have a hard time finding a viewer benefit in a story, then maybe that story doesn't belong in the newscast. Analyzing whether there is a hook is a good test for a story.

Avoid long leads. You're bombarded with long lead sentences in newspaper copy and wire copy. Most newspaper leads try to include all the important details of a story. However, in television news you shouldn't put all the facts in a single lead sentence. Your viewers will have a hard time understanding long sentences. Weave all the important facts through your story.

Keep the lead timely. An advantage of television news is time. Stations broadcast virtually around the clock now. If something happens in the morning, it has to be made current in the early evening newscasts.

BAD: "Four people were injured this morning when their minivan skidded into a guard rail on the Interstate in heavy rains."

BETTER: "Members of a Michigan family are still in University Hospital at this hour. All four were seriously injured in an accident on the Interstate during this morning's heavy rains."

Story Structure

There is another major difference between writing for the ear and writing for the eye. You may have been told in writing a story to tell readers what you are going to tell them, tell them, and then tell them what you told them. This works well in a book or a magazine, but not in writing broadcast news. Good broadcast stories have a beginning, middle and end. Each section of the story serves a specific purpose.

The beginning. Every story needs a point, a hook that provides a clear focus. The start of a story tells the viewer what it is all about. It creates a focus and gives the viewer a reason to be interested in the story.

The middle. Since you can't put all the details of the story in the first sentences, develop the story in the middle section. The middle provides the details of the lead and answers the viewers' questions. Limit yourself to two or three important points.

The end. Don't end a story without a conclusion. Wrap it up by repeating the most important point, the viewer benefit, or what development to expect next. One of the worst clichés at the end of a story is: "The cause is still under investigation." It doesn't tell the audience anything. Instead, try something like: "Police still don't know what caused the crash. They expect test reports back on Friday. We'll have them for you then."

Basic Rules

Power producers also master the basic rules of broadcast news copy. These writing rules have a common goal, to make a story easier to understand. Also, these rules give the anchor and reporter a fair chance to read their copy on air without mistake.

Numbers. Make the anchor's job easier when writing numbers. Always spell out numbers from one to eleven. Use numerals for all other numbers, but always spell out thousands, millions, and billions. Round off large numbers. Instead of 255-thousand 482 dollars and 18 cents, just write 255-thousand-dollars. Dollar is spelled out, as are numbers with fractions or decimal points. For instance, a quarter of a million-dollars or one-point-five-billion-dollars. Years are an exception. Anchors quickly understand a year such as 1952, so use numerals for years.

Abbreviations. Spell out all abbreviations as you want them read on air. If the abbreviation is to be read as an abbreviation on the air, then separate the letters with a hyphen, as in U-A-W or C-I-A. If an acronym is well known, then leave it in the copy, as with NATO or OPEC. But, be careful with abbreviations and acronyms. If there is any doubt in your mind that the public won't easily understand the abbreviation, then use the full name. It's safer and protects your anchor from a possible stumble.

Punctuation. Don't use elaborate punctuation in broadcast news copy. Don't use colons or semicolons. Even commas aren't always used in broadcast copy to designate a pause or change in thought. Many anchors prefer the triple periods of an ellipsis (...) to designate a pause because it is easier to read on the TelePrompTer.

Quotations. Direct quotations are rare in broadcast copy. Actually, you should be using a video sound bite if the statement is important enough. If you don't have the sound bite, then paraphrase. Paraphrasing is easier to understand. If it's important to use an exact quote, then set it up with a line like "in her own words" or "as she put it." Never write quote ... unquote. This is confusing.

Names. Always keep names and titles simple and conversational. If you have to identify someone by title, then put the title ahead of the name as you would for attribution. Add any identifying information after the name. Don't string out titles into a long line of words. For example, "Syracuse University associate professor of broadcast journalism Fred Furd says ..." is too long. Use instead, "Journalism professor Fred Furd says ..." and then identify his school in the next sentence.

Pronunciation. The news is full of unfamiliar names, particularly in international stories. Include a pronunciation guide on difficult names

---

> **TIP — IMPORTANT QUOTES**
> Create a full-screen graphic of a quote when it's crucial to a story.

in copy for your anchors. The wires carry pronunciation guides and update them daily. Put the pronouncer after the name in the copy, as in "Russian peace envoy Viktor Chernomyrdin (chehr-nuh-MEER-din) says ..." or "New refugees crossed the border at Blace (BLAH - tsyuh)."

Also be alert to regional pronunciation differences like Nevada (Naa-vah-da), the state, and Nevada (Naa-vay-da), the Missouri town. Another example is Greenwich. In New York State it's Greenwich (Green-witch), and in Connecticut it's Greenwich (Gren-itch). There must be hundreds of such cases to bedevil producers, anchors and weathercasters.

Spelling. A misspelled word can easily trip up an anchor. Although anchors are supposed to read their copy before they go on air, you know sloppy anchors who aren't careful about reviewing the script. If they hit a misspelled word, they could stumble.

Grammar. Bad grammar also can throw off your anchors and make them look bad. A phrase like, "Now the news kids is waiting for ..." does nothing to enhance your anchors' authority. What about the reporter who says, "Two twins were found dead in this house tonight." Was it one pair of twins or two sets of twins? Protect your anchor and your reporters by checking copy for bad grammar.

Writing to Video

Watch out for wallpaper. Wallpaper refers to pictures that aren't connected to the anchor copy. Sportscasters use this a lot. You've seen video of unidentified players running up and down a field or court. Over the picture the sportscaster is talking about a specific player who has just been traded or who has signed a contract. Unfortunately, you have no idea which player is in the news because the sportscaster never makes a specific reference to the video. The trouble is, wallpaper is easy to create. Without looking at it, you take some video off the network satellite feed or from a photographer, hand it to a tape editor, and ask them to cut :30 seconds. You do all this even before you've written a script. Without specific instructions, the editor lays down :30 seconds of random video. You'll have no hope of the pictures matching your script. Fortunately, with a little time and attention to detail, wallpaper is an easy problem to correct. You should look at the video and make a shot log, then talk with the editor about the best shots, write those shots into your script, and then share your script with the editor so she can edit to your copy.

Don't write too closely. Writing too closely is the opposite of wallpaper, when the copy hugs the pictures to death. In this case the writer doing the story describes every single shot or scene in the edited video. You don't see this problem as frequently as video wallpaper, but it happens. Such writing isn't interesting and not good television.

Go for the hit and run. This is the best way to write to video. You write specifically to the video, describing what's going on: a hit. At other times in your script you don't describe what the viewers are seeing because the action is self-evident or not important: a run. When you write to the specific scene or shot, try to make a point for the viewers.

Make sure the video sequence is logical. A video sequence is a series of shots edited to demonstrate a process or shorten the length of an action. You show the viewers what happened or demonstrate how something works. You don't need to describe every detail because the audience also can see what is happening.

Don't forget the sound. Sometimes producers forget how well sound augments video and helps bring a story alive. Perhaps the best example of what not to do is show a band in a parade without music. Remember that even video in voice-overs benefits from natural sound, or "natsot." A little natsot brings life to a voice-over or package.

Writing Tips

Writing great broadcast copy is tough work, but these final tips will go a long way in helping you become a power producer.

Read aloud. Read your copy aloud as you go along, and then after you finish the script. This is the best possible way to identify mistakes. You'll find wording that is tough to read on the air. You'll be amazed at what you find with this simple step.

Use action verbs. Make your verbs exciting. John doesn't just hit the ball, he smashes or slams it. But avoid clichés.

Avoid pronouns. It's too hard for the listener to follow when you refer to an earlier noun. Repeat the noun even if it seems awkward to the eye.

Watch your adjectives. Avoid adjectives used on tabloid shows. How do you know a city is in mourning or is shocked or is horrified? Exaggerated and inaccurate words discredit your copy. Eventually the audience will realize your news is only providing cheap emotionalism.

Don't assume. When writing news copy, make sure you understand the story. Make no assumptions: To use a cliché (sorry), assumptions can make an ASS of U and ME! Read the source copy carefully and check on anything you don't understand.

Write transitions. Write meaningful transitions between stories. This helps the viewer move from story to story. Avoid "meanwhile," "elsewhere," and "in other news," however. Also, don't force a transition between two stories with no connection.

Don't be lazy. Rewrite! The "dup" key is found on some older newsroom computer systems, like BASYS. It allows you to copy a story from one newscast and drop it in another show. The newer computer software allows you to copy stories using cut and paste. Either way, this is a bad idea. Why take a story from one show and insert it verbatim in another? This isn't providing the audience with fresh news. In fact, this practice is the mark of journeyman producers. It's a clear indication that they don't respect their audience enough to

Interview: News Director

Willie Chriesman
News Director
WVTM-TV
Birmingham, AL

Willie Chriesman began his producing career while still in high school in Birmingham. After graduating from Northwestern University with a journalism degree, Chriesman joined CNN as a writer and producer. He went on to produce at WLS-TV in Chicago and WDIV-TV in Detroit. He joined news management as executive producer at KCNC-TV in Denver, later becoming executive producer of the Fox News Service. Before joining WVTM-TV in 1997, he was assistant news director at WCVB-TV in Boston.

Why did you become a producer when you started out? What attracted you to producing?

I think everyone starts out thinking they should be on the air. Then they get into a newsroom and see there's more to it than that. It occurred to me that there were roles that, for lack of a better word, had more power. They had more influence on the product itself. Producing seemed to be the most influential position to aspire to. And it also seemed that it was a good career path as well. It also struck me early on that on-air people, or people who want to be on-air, are pretty easy to find. There is much more value in producers, and producers probably have more job security than anyone else in the newsroom.

How well-prepared were you when you became a producer? You were relatively young weren't you?

The first newscast I produced was when I was still in high school and an intern at WBRC-TV in Birmingham. I used to work weekends; that was when there really were no weekend producers in this market. The anchors produced their own newscasts. They were happy to have a little help and have someone sit in the booth and watch things for them. The transition was fairly easy because it was the weekend and the environment wasn't high pressure.

What was the toughest part of the job as you became a full-time producer?

The toughest part is to be creative and to think about how you are going to make this newscast stand out. You always hear from prospective employers that they aren't looking for "stackers," and that's a concept that's hard to grasp at first. Eventually you rewrite the story or add new information.

Beware the split screen. Newsroom computer systems allow you to split the computer screen so you can look at the wire story on one side and write your own copy on the other. Although this saves time, it can also be a trap. If you aren't careful you'll find yourself rearranging the words from the wire copy and the result will be journalese.

Don't split words or sentences. When writing broadcast copy, never split a word between lines. Splitting a word using a hyphen is too difficult for an anchor to read. Also, for the same reason, never split sentences between pages.

Now you've got the basic rules of writing conversational broadcast copy, the five C's. However, if you are going to be a power producer, you need to remain a student of the craft. Constantly check your writing and keep honing your skills. Newswriting is an important skill, so it is important that you read and review books on broadcast newswriting. Read one at least once a year. There is no better way to recover from journalese. You'll find books on news writing listed in Resources for Producers at the end of this handbook.

Now it's time to move on to the third major role of the power producer, that of creating the newscast.

---

understand that what you are trying to create is a television program. So, sometimes it was hard to figure out what a stacker is and why you don't want to do that. What a producer should be doing is to craft not only the stories but also how the stories are told and how they are produced. Your first goal as a producer is to get the thing on the air and off the air and make sure all the commercials run. But as you go along you want to do more and become more of a craftsperson. That's the toughest part of it.

What do you know now that you wish you knew when you were first starting out as a young producer in Birmingham?

The demands on a producer when I started were fairly limited. When I began doing weekend newscasts in Birmingham in the mid-1970s, we didn't have reporters, so we didn't have to make decisions about who covered what. The most challenging thing was to figure out which piece to take off the affiliate feed from ABC. Not to date myself, but I started in a simpler time. The challenges producers face today are much more daunting. It's not so much cut and paste now. There are so many elements—production and graphics and satellite technology—that were never an issue for me when I was growing up.

What do you look for when you hire producers?

I promise not to use the words "think outside the box." You want someone who thinks of the newscast as, what I call a "living, breathing organism." You want someone who can go with the flow, who can make changes, who can see something increase or decrease in value as the newscast grows. It is never set in stone. Ultimately you want somebody who is flexible, who thinks about the "big picture." (Sorry, I had to slip in one cliché.) You want somebody who understands that his or her newscast is part of an overall effort. Also, someone who responds well to breaking news and the pressures that come with that.

What advice do you have for entry-level producers?

Some things need to be instinct for them. They need to be people who not only love news but also love television. They should never lose sight of the fact that they are putting on a television program and that it is competing in an environment where people have dozens of choices. Producers have to think about what they are offering viewers, and they need to know what would make viewers give up their time to watch that newscast. Good producers need to be students of television as well as the events around them. They need to take from those experiences and observations so they can put on a distinctive product, a newscast that stands out. Again, you want to put on a newscast that cuts through the clutter. You want to use whatever tools are available, trying new things every day. The audience isn't getting any bigger and won't be growing anytime soon. So we really need to put on a responsible yet compelling product every day of the week.

Chapter 6

Role Three: Production Expert

Building the News Show

In This Chapter:

- The Basic Framework
- The Lead
- The Open
- The Blocks
- Story Count and Flow
- The Close

Chapter 6:
Building the News Show

"To be a power producer, you must thoroughly understand the newscast structure, the format and how to pull it together."

Put 10 producers in a room and give them a list of 20 stories. Then ask them to create a rundown, a basic lineup of news stories. What will you get? You'll have 10 different rundowns.

Crafting a newscast is a creative process, full of decisions based on all seven producer roles. In creating a newscast you function as a journalist, news writer, production expert, promotion writer, team leader, researcher and lawyer/ethicist.

To be a power producer, you must thoroughly understand the newscast structure, the format and how to pull it together. You must master how to build a newscast. This means you must know what makes a good lead story, what goes in the different blocks or segments, and what is a strong close. You need to master basic producing concepts like story count, pace, flow and moments. This is all part of the creativity of producing, and it keeps the audience involved. The goal of this chapter is to help you master this process.

The Basic Framework

Over the last 30 years, television and cable newsrooms have developed a basic framework for newscasts.

The format. This framework, or format, is fairly standard. For instance, newscasts need news blocks to separate the commercial breaks so the newscast isn't cluttered with too many commercials all at once. Despite what those in your sales department might think, there is a limit to how many commercials you can put in a newscast without driving away viewers.

Formats vary, however, depending on the length of the newscast and the time of day. For instance, the format for a straight hour is different from that for a half-hour broadcast. Format also depends on the time of the newscast, because the time of day often dictates the particular viewer's lifestyle and level of news interest.

The rundown. Your rundown is a list of stories arranged in a logical sequence that you create on the newsroom computer system. This rundown becomes your news and production road map. In the hours leading up to the newscast, you and the newscast production team use it to organize such tasks as writing the script, setting priorities for tape editing and graphics, and setting times for each story. It outlines every detail of the newscast as we'll see in Chapter 8.

The Lead

Every rundown needs an effective lead story to provide a strong launch and attract viewers to your newscast. Without a strong lead you're telling the viewers nothing important happened today and that there is no reason to stay tuned.

In developing a rundown, picking a lead story is the most important decision you make. News directors, news managers and producers all agonize over having the best lead. As the producer, you may not make the final decision on a lead. Because it's so critical, the news director in many newsrooms has the final say in deciding the lead.

Enterprising the lead. One way to ensure that you have a powerful lead story every day is through planning. Why wait for a lead story to suddenly emerge from daily news events? Enterprise reporting and preplanning creates a more effective lead. It's a story you have and the competition doesn't. It can also target your newscast's audience. The enterprise lead gives your audience a unique story as well as a promotable reason for viewers to keep watching.

The point is, don't leave your lead story to the news gods. Don't wait until that morning to start developing a potential lead story. Plan the lead as many days in advance as possible. Working ahead gives your reporters a chance to develop different angles and to produce a story that makes your coverage memorable. At the same time, make changes if a stronger story develops during the news day.

Developing the lead. There's endless debate on what makes the best lead story. However, everyone agrees that a strong lead grabs as many viewers as possible. An effective lead hits viewers emotionally as well as intellectually, and touches their lives. It should also be what the news business calls a water-cooler story, a story people will be talking about at work.

Lead stories need to be carefully developed. In a single word, produced. This is why power producers spend time working on their lead stories. They make sure all the elements of the story are covered, and present it so viewers can easily understand why this story is the lead.

Packaging the lead. There are several ways to package the lead to make it clearly important. The most popular ways are the big story or team coverage. To make a lead story a big story, the packaging must be big. Make the lead story more than a single report. Develop other stories to put this event into context or add the human dimension. Another way to showcase a series of stories tied to the lead is through team coverage or a team report. As you read in Chapter 4, when you build a team report, you assign different aspects of a major story to different reporters.

Give all stories related to the lead report a graphic label like "Top Story." Other on-screen graphics could include a banner and a common title for the stories, or a common graphic designed to highlight in-depth coverage. Also, pull the coverage together with your copy.

A common way to sell a lead story has the reporter live from the story location. However, before you automatically do a live report on your lead, you need to deal with the challenge of making a live report interesting. How visually interesting is a live report from the scene of a story hours after the event, when nothing is happening? Pointless or dull live reports are a major viewer complaint.

One of the laws of producing is to get to your video as quickly as possible. When you put the reporter on camera first, you delay getting to actual video of the story. Traditionally, your anchors do an on-camera lead-in to the reporter. Then, you go to the reporter live and he or she does another lead-in to the package. All this delays getting to the first video.

Getting to your first news video can take even longer if you're going to a live network report, a so called "o-one feed." These reports are timed to start at exactly 30 seconds or one minute after the hour so stations all over the nation can use the report live. While this type of report is valuable, it means that at the start of the newscast your anchors read a minute or more of copy before the network's report. One solution is to use the best video as an anchor voice-over in the lead-in to the live report or network feed.

Other types of leads. Of course, some days you have an embarrassment of riches, or more than one good lead story. Or you can have the opposite problem, no clear lead. In either case, you can use what's called an umbrella lead. Lead with a quick headline and pictures, promise more on that story in a moment, and then go into another big story. Of course, the other lead story follows immediately.

There is another issue for producers when it comes to selecting a lead. This is the potential conflict with news shows scheduled back to back. Years ago, the conventional wisdom was to with-

TIP

WHAT MAKES A GOOD LEAD?

As you make your decision on a lead, look for specific ingredients.
- Is the story local or does it have local impact, such as job cuts by the largest local employer?
- Does the story directly touch the lives of your viewers?
- If a story doesn't directly affect some viewers, is it of such weight that they still need to know about it?
- Is this story part of a local or national trend, for example contradictory reports on the value of mammograms in detecting breast cancer.
- Is this story so new that the audience didn't read it in the morning paper or see it on the station's last newscast?
- Does the story contain human drama?

TIP

LEAD LOCAL

There is a rule in local television news that you should always try to lead your newscast with a local story. However, most rules are made to be broken, with good reason. In one market, a producer originally created a rundown with the opening of a new supermarket as the lead. This was an important local news story in a community with economic problems. However, this was also the day the Monica Lewinsky story broke. Ultimately, the news director overruled the producer. The lesson is that you need to weigh your lead story options carefully and not just go blindly by a rule.

hold a big story until the 6 o'clock newscast. Today, this isn't the case. Producers can't short-change those who watch the earlier newscasts. However, you do want to maintain the audience's interest by selecting different leads. So, in keeping with the audience demographics, lead the first half-hour newscast with a story that appeals to that specific audience, but give the story a different treatment in the next half hour.

For example, the 5 p.m. lead might be a medical treatment for women developed at a local hospital. This is a good lead since the early evening audience is weighted more toward women. Give the story the full treatment with the medical reporter live from the hospital. At 5:30 p.m., come back with a brief story with voice-over as part of the medical franchise. At 6 p.m., go back to the report as a major story, but with a different treatment.

The Open

Newscasts must start as strongly as possible. Not only does your newscast need a strong lead, you also need a pre-produced tape open and pre-show teases to grab the audience. While the headline teases entice viewers to stay tuned, the open sets the tone and style of the newscast. It introduces your anchors and other major talent. In fact, the open is really a promo for your station's news image. It establishes your news marketing position such as, "We've got you covered," or "Live, local, late breaking." The open should match the graphic and news style of the station.

Newscast opens come in a variety of forms and styles. Some show the anchors' pictures or the names of local communities to give a sense of local news coverage.

Opens don't open. In many newscasts, the open doesn't begin the broadcast—instead it comes at the end of the first block, with only a cursory mention of the anchors' names at the start of the newscast. Moving the open into the newscast allows the program to get to the news faster, with a better chance of holding the lead-in audience. This is sometimes called a "restart."

Seamless breaks. Over the years power

TIP: KEEP IT SHORT

Don't try to dazzle the audience with your open. You don't have time. Remember the viewer is probably holding a remote control. Get to your lead story as quickly as possible.

producers have learned you need to get into the newscast as quickly as possible to hold the lead-in audience. The best way to accomplish this is to use a seamless break. This means there are no commercials between the lead-in or lead-out programs and the newscast.

One way to get from the lead-in program to your newscast as quickly as possible is to do your pre-show teases with the credits of the preceding program. To aid their affiliated stations, the networks now allow stations to do their pre-show teases using a split screen in which your local anchors share the screen with the closing credits of the lead-in program. If you don't have a network program before your newscast, suggest doing the same thing with the syndicated program.

The Blocks

Once your newscast is launched, the next step is filling the blocks. This is the time between commercial breaks. These blocks are the time available, the news hole, for news, sports and weather.

The way blocks are named and numbered varies. The most popular method is to designate each block by a letter, so you have an A block, B block, etc. Some newsrooms use a numbering system. All the first block stories start with 1 and can go on to page 19, then all the second block stories start with the number 2, the first story is 21, the next 22, and so on. Today, computer systems already come with a rundown template that designates the page numbers by letter. No matter how they're designated, each block actually plays a specific role in your newscast.

The A block. This is the most important block because it gets the viewers involved in the newscast. For that reason, this segment runs longer than any other block. The idea is to keep viewers from clicking away to the competition. This practice is called front-loading. Some stations actually promote long first blocks through "10 at 10" or 11 at 11," promising 10 or 11 minutes of news before the first break. Some stations treat the A block as a mini-newscast. It has a strong lead story, perhaps another major local story, along with quick local and national headlines packaged as a fast-paced digest. At the end of the block, these mini-newscasts feature a brief weathercast, maybe sports headlines, followed by a memorable story before the teases and video open.

The B block. This is the block where you run more news, but also special reports or franchises. Promoting these at the end of the A block should hold your viewers through the commercials. Start the B block with a story that's almost as important as the lead story. Since you always tease the next story after the break, this must be a significant story. Try to start this block with strong video and never lead with a reader.

The weather block. Weather is often more important than the rest of the news. Researchers find emergency weather and weather reporting score at the top of the list when they ask viewers what is important. This makes sense because weather has a direct impact every day on our lives. Exact placement of the weather block varies, but weather is so important the news director decides this.

The sports block. On the other hand, the sports segment is of low interest. Audience research puts sports at the bottom. Sports fans are usually younger male viewers, and low television news viewers. However, it is vital you cover sports. Advertisers love sports because of those younger male viewers.

Power producers try to place strong news stories around sports and weather. The best stories are those related to weather or sports. A voice-over of severe weather such as a tornado or hurricane in another region provides a valuable lead to the local weather segment. Also, using a sports-related story, such as a stadium bond issue, in the sports-block broadens the interest in sports.

Other blocks. Of course, not all newscasts are produced in a simple progression of blocks. One variation is to put a commercial break in the middle of weather or sports. It's not a bad idea to have the weathercaster stop before a break and tease that he'll be back with the "Full action track storm threat Doppler 99,000 forecast" next. You also can split sports with a break. Separating your breaks this way allows you to put additional news around these two segments.

The last block. The last block of a newscast includes the final story, the anchors' goodbye and the tease to the next newscast. You can also include a recap of the top stories or provide late information on breaking stories reported earlier, or at least remind viewers that you'll have more information in the next newscast.

This last block is a good place to remind the audience about any telephone numbers you've given them during the show, and repeat those numbers with a super or graphic. Try to make this a regular feature. This serves your viewers and shows them you go that extra step to help them. Repeating the weather forecast, particularly for the next school day, is another viewer service. Parents want to know how to dress the kids in the morning.

Another possible last block element is a look at the big stories you'll be covering the next day. People want not just what has happened but also what is going to happen. Include a brief digest of scheduled news for the next day and potential follow-up stories. It's smart promotion and gives the viewers a reason to watch tomorrow.

Longer newscasts. While similar in many ways to half-hour news programs, hour-long newscasts need special format considerations. The long-held theory by programmers is that the audience tends to change channels on the hour, although this may no longer be true because of remote controls. Still, an hour newscast, particularly one that starts at 5 o'clock, will usually have a second lead at 5:30, preceded by some sort of supertease to hold viewers for the next half hour. In an hour newscast you might not slot franchise reports until the C block or later in the newscast. While you may only do sports once in an hour, you may have two or three weather segments. Holding viewers for the full hour takes a special attention to teases, and they help dictate how you format a newscast. An hour show needs a strong story at the end of the hour because you tease it at the end of the A block, and at several other points throughout the newscast.

Story Count and Flow

Power producers take into consideration some of the finer points in producing as they block out the newscast.

Story count. A major consideration in creating your rundown is a hotly debated newsroom issue: story count. As a producer, your job is to balance in-depth reporting against the audiences' desire for a headline service and a fast-paced newscast to hold their attention. There are ways you can balance these competing interests. One effective way to increase story count is through quick digests of world, national or regional headlines.

Pacing. Closely tied to story count is the pace of your newscast. Pace refers to the tempo of your newscast. You create a rhythm to your newscast through the length and treatment of the stories. Shorter stories mean a faster pace. Ask producers and they'll tell you they like fast-paced newscasts, but talk to a viewer and the answer is different. Viewers say they miss information when a show is too fast-paced. The correct pace depends on your station's news image and strategy. For example, if you're an Action News station, then the pacing will be quick with short stories. Most stations today, no matter the name, are really variations on the Eyewitness format. This format means a slower pace with longer live and on-set reports.

Producers have a number of devices they can use to speed up or slow down the pace of a newscast. You can speed up the pace by changing anchors frequently, using brief copy stories or headline digests. Another pacing device is to go directly to your weather and sports segments with no anchor toss, and by eliminating other places in the newscast with anchor happy talk or crosstalk. You also can help pacing by constantly changing graphics and using animated opens with audio stingers for special reports and franchises. Changing anchors after every story creates a ping-pong effect, which most news directors and viewers don't like. However, some faster paced and more tabloid newscasts use anchor ping-pong to step up pacing.

Flow. To help hold viewers, producers try to arrange stories in a logical sequence. Grouping stories based on a common topic or viewer interest creates flow. For example, group the stories on education together. Normally the same anchor reads all these related stories. You change anchors when the subject changes.

Say you have a package from a local reporter

> **WARNING!**
> **CHEAP AND CHEESY**
>
> Don't over-reach trying to create a newscast moment and do something cheap and cheesy. The best moments are honest with real emotion. The audience realizes when you try to manipulate emotions, and doesn't like it.

on an education story and two wire stories on statewide education issues. Start with the package, go to the copy story, and try to do the third story as a voice-over. Try to keep the same anchor through the grouping, but change the anchor if you have too many related stories together. Change anchors any time you feel you are asking an anchor to read too much or are stretching the audiences' interest.

If a string of stories is just too long, then consider taking a couple of stories and moving them elsewhere in the newscast to a different block. Sometimes in a local newscast you'll see anchors read a long series of related stories, often on a subject like crime. This is weak producing because after a couple of stories the audience is probably losing interest.

Also, in orchestrating the flow of stories, don't forget transition lines between a group of stories or related stories. Of course you don't want to use weak transition lines such as "in related medical news" or "in another crime story." One solution is to change anchors when two stories don't work well together and there is no natural transition.

Moments. Moments are stories or interactions you build into the newscast that you hope the audience will find memorable. Try to find something that will touch the viewer. The audience will remember a moment long after everything else in the newscast is forgotten. Your viewers are looking for something with sincere meaning. An example is a dog up for adoption during a regular pet franchise. Another memorable moment could be something out of the ordinary, such as a package about a new treatment for a disease, followed by a live interview with a local person whose life was saved by this treatment.

The Close

Your newscast must end with a strong finish. Too often producers allow the final few minutes of a newscast to be an afterthought. However, this closing block is incredibly important. This block sets the tone for how the audience remembers your program.

The final story. The final story may be the second most important story of the day after the lead story. Even so, producers, reporters and assignment editors often treat it as an afterthought. They spend a good deal of the morning news meeting talking about a potential lead story, but seldom work on finding a good closing story.

Power producers know the value of a strong closing story. It's a story you can tease during the newscast, and you need a strong tease to keep non-sports fans through the sportscast. Another reason for a strong final story is that your audience needs to leave your newscast feeling the time they spent watching was time well spent.

The last story is often called the kicker. This can mean a funny story you think the audience will remember. However, the kicker doesn't have to be funny. Offbeat, interesting, memorable or even emotional stories all work. Another approach is to close with a local entertainment report from a feature reporter. In any event, this last story should be the kind of story people will be talking about around the water cooler the next day. If your newsroom doesn't pay attention to the need for a strong final story, you must look through the lineups from the various feeds and try to find a kicker story. Don't end up with a meaningless VNR like a water skiing squirrel from Florida. It's not interesting and certainly not local.

Any good story, song, symphony or book has a strong finish. Orchestrate your newscast by looking for a way to bring the newscast to a strong close. Don't just allow the newscast to drift away in a hurried good night because you can't back-time properly. This is unfair to your newsroom and makes the anchors look uncomfortable. Finish your newscast with as much finesse as you've put into the rest of it.

No matter how well you build your news broadcast, unless you've considered the time of the day the newscast airs, you're in trouble. The time your broadcast airs determines the format and content, because the viewing audience changes dramatically hour by hour. In the next chapter, you'll find out how to produce for different audiences in different time periods.

Chapter 7

Role Three: Production Expert

The Newscast Format

In This Chapter:

- The Audience
- The Time Element
- Formats
- Consultants

Chapter 7: The Newscast Format

> "Each broadcast has its own style and format based on the time it runs and the audience's lifestyle during that time slot."

As you put your newscast together, it's absolutely crucial that you understand the viewing habits and demographics of your audience.

At one time, you didn't have to worry too much about things like audience composition. Virtually everyone in the family gathered around the set in the living room and watched that night's newscast. They got their television news from The Huntley-Brinkley Report on NBC or The CBS Evening News with Walter Cronkite. People did the same thing with their local news.

Today, "appointment viewing" is almost gone. For one thing, families no longer gather to watch television. Television sets are in the kitchen, the den, the family room, the bedroom and even the bathroom. There is no longer an hour set aside for news viewing.

As a producer, you must take into account today's viewing environment. That environment has been profoundly changed by the audience, technology and the competition. You can't afford to produce yesterday's newscast for today's audience.

The Audience

Your basic assumptions about the audience need to be tested. Today, there is no longer a typical audience; in fact each newscast has a different audience. Also, the importance of each newscast has changed as viewing patterns have changed.

Not only have viewing patterns changed, but the kind of news these viewers need has changed. Some of these changes include more two- or three-income families, more women working outside the home, and people working longer hours. These changes in the workforce mean more people watch early-morning newscasts. Also, as more people move from traditional manufacturing jobs to knowledge-based jobs, their news interests change.

Today's audience is busier and more easily distracted. They don't always pay close attention to your broadcast. Larry Rickel's Broadcast Image Group put a camera in a kitchen next to a television set to demonstrate how a family watches local news. Needless to say, the family didn't watch but listened to the television. However, they did stop and pay attention when interested! Your challenge is to get these viewers to pay more attention.

The Time Element

When a newscast aired was always important, but it is even moreso now. Power producers understand that each broadcast has its own style and format based on the time it runs and the audience's lifestyle during that time slot. You need to understand these differences.

Early evening. Stations today run a string of newscasts from late afternoon through early evening. The idea is to take advantage of the audience lead-in from strong programs like The Oprah Winfrey Show and The Rosie O'Donnell Show, or use a local news program as the lead-in for the next local newscast.

The audience changes through each half hour of the early evening. Demographics change from an older and mostly female audience to a more balanced audience by 6 p.m. However, with people working longer hours and getting home later, the early news still lacks young adult viewers compared to the late news audience.

The earlier the newscast, the more likely you'll have women-oriented franchises, like consumer and medical reports. Harder edged investigative and crime solver franchises belong in the later half hours, along with sports, when there are more male viewers.

Many news people still tend to think of the

early evening newscast as the most important. However, in many major markets, the ratings for these newscasts have dropped dramatically. While at one time the early evening news was the local newscast of record, this is no longer true. Still, you get arguments from reporters who feel that their story is so important it should air in what they view as the flagship newscast.

"Habit viewers" are still a component of the early news ratings. These viewers watch the same newscast and anchor team night after night. These habit viewers tend to be older, even elderly.

Late news. Even though the ratings are sometimes not as high for the late news as the early news, this still may be the most important newscast. This audience is better balanced demographically with almost as many men as women, and younger and older viewers. This audience attracts advertisers, and a station can normally charge more for the late news. Unfortunately, there is less commercial time available in the 35-minute late news.

What kind of news is this audience looking for? They want new news. They don't want a sloppy update or a repackaging of the early evening newscast. They want to know what has happened since the early news. Headlines are sufficient to give these viewers an understanding of what happened earlier while they were at work.

Ratings for the late news are dependent in many ways on network lead-in programs. This is one reason you are asked to run stories that relate to successful lead-in programming. The sign of a strong local news operation is one that does well in the late news ratings despite a weak network.

Fox and independent stations have been highly successful with 10 p.m. and 9 p.m. newscasts. At first they did well in the ratings because of the convenience of news an hour before the affiliates. Now these stations are drawing viewers because the newscasts appeal to younger viewers.

Mornings. Just 15 years ago, the mornings were an afterthought in most newsrooms. Now, with people going to work earlier and earlier, this time period is highly valuable. The morning audi-

TIP
THE TIME TO START CHANGES

The conventional wisdom is that the late news is the first place a station can begin to improve its news ratings. Because late news viewers are younger and less likely to be habit viewers, they tend to be more open to on-air changes. The late news is often where a station introduces a new anchor team or a new format.

ence now ranks third in the pecking order of daily newscasts, ahead of the traditional noon news.

Since viewers are just getting ready for a new day, your format must fit their activities. They only have so much time to watch your news. In fact, they are really listening. This is why you format 15- to 20-minute news blocks. Early morning viewers are looking for quick headlines. Because they go to bed early, they typically don't watch the late news so they want to know what has happened since last night's early news. Late sports scores are important, but the most critical news is the weather forecast. Viewers want to know what the weather is going to be like.

Noon. At one time the noon newscast was important. Yes, the ratings still might be good, but older habit viewers drive them. The audience is mostly women, what the Nielsen books label as W50+, not the most popular audience for advertisers. This viewer profile has a big impact on the format and style of the noon. Noon newscasts tend to be more of a friendly visit than a hard-edged newscast.

Weekends. Stations are guilty of treating weekends as a stepchild. Again, the ratings are driven more by lead-in than habit and loyalty. Still, the late newscast on Sunday evening usually has excellent ratings. People want to catch up on what happened over the weekend and hear the next day's weather forecast.

Formats

In the early years, both local and national newscasts resembled each other. The story count was low and the pace slow, but the news was often compelling. Now, local newscasts are no longer clones of the networks. Stations are trying to give people a reason to watch their newscasts. Local producers have changed their newscasts to reflect their own audience. Over the years a variety of news formats have evolved.

Traditional. At one time, when local news was more a public service than a money maker, stations split the news into three blocks of news, sports and weather. Stories were grouped based on national, international and local. It was unsophisticated. A white male anchored these traditional newscasts with white guys also doing sports and weather. My particular favorite was the weather segment, sponsored by a gasoline company, that featured the weather person dressed as a service station attendant. Yes, each block was usually sponsored. Sometimes the sponsor's name was prominently displayed on the anchor desk, a practice seen as ethically questionable today.

Eyewitness News. The good old days ended in the late '60s when broadcast station groups discovered they could make money in local news. In fact, a great deal of money. This increased pressure on news departments to generate ratings, so station owners started to provide resources in terms of people and equipment.

One such group was Westinghouse, then known as Group W. They pioneered a new style of local news called Eyewitness News. Group W stations hired reporters who went out to cover stories and used film to describe the event. Another change was when news directors like Al Primo had the idea of putting reporters on the set and talking with the anchors. These reporters began to become more important and the anchors had to learn to ask questions.

Primo later became news director at WABC-TV in New York. There he further developed the Eyewitness News format with star reporters like Geraldo Rivera, Ernie Anastos, Joan Lunden, Sal Marchiano, and RoseAnn Scamardella, all of whom worked with the anchor team of Roger Grimsby and Bill Beutel. Grimsby brought humor and personality to the anchor chair. Critics called this style happy talk.

Grimsby was joined in other markets by similar strong personalities, many on ABC-owned stations, like Bill Bonds on WXYZ-TV in Detroit, Van Amburg on KGO-TV in San Francisco, and Fahey Flynn and Joel Daly on WLS-TV in Chicago. The ABC-owned stations went from a weak third in the ratings to dominating their markets.

Local stations also realized, with the help of consultants and audience research, that the single white male anchor failed to represent the audience. Working with the Eyewitness format, they found that co-anchors helped the pace and flow of the newscasts, particularly when producing an hour-long newscast. Local stations promoted women to this co-anchor chair. In some markets the woman anchor became the most important anchor in the market, such as Monica Kaufman in Atlanta, Ann Bishop in Miami, Jean Enersen in Seattle, and Natalie Jacobson in Boston.

Today, most stations are doing some variation of the Eyewitness approach. They may call it Newswatch, Newsbeat, or a variety of names, but the format is based on the Eyewitness format.

Action News. This alternative to the Eyewitness format came from WPVI in Philadelphia. The station is famous for brief copy, high story count, and spot news. WPVI's owners, Capital Cities, used the same format to build successful newscasts in Buffalo and Houston. At one time, WCPO-TV in Cincinnati was also known for a similar format of brief film stories with dramatic music.

Franchise news. A franchise-heavy newscast, called "News You Can Use," is a variation of the Eyewitness newscast. As you know, franchises use featured reporters or anchors to cover topics important to local viewers. While some newscasts have more franchises than others, most incorporate some form of such special reporting. The most popular franchises are medicine and consumer news, because these subjects score well in viewer research. But there are other franchises, including parenting, crime fighting, pets, Internet sites, and consumer action lines like "7 on Your Side." All are designed to meet some viewer interest.

The promotion department drives this franchise format. Promotion wants the audience to know that your newscast reports on topics of high interest. It's hard to carve out a unique marketing position for your newscast against competing stations based on having franchises. Virtually all stations do franchises. However, franchises are now something the audience expects. To stay competitive, your news department needs to develop at least some local franchises targeted at your audience.

Franchise reporters are considered sub-anchors, and appear regularly on the news set. At other times, news directors ask major anchors or potential anchors to do a franchise. Some franchise reporters have become stars in the their own right such as Marvin Zindler, consumer reporter at KTRK-TV in Houston. Zindler is best known for his white suits, white hair, tinted sun glasses, and his role in breaking a story that became a musical and movie, "The Best Little Whorehouse in Texas."

Community helper. While using the Eyewitness format, some stations have positioned themselves as community service stations. Most stations today invest in community projects and outreach efforts because they're good for their local news image. One Minneapolis station known for community involvement even changed its call letters to KARE-TV.

Tabloid news. Of course there have been other successful local news formats. From time to time stations have used a tabloid approach based on entertainment news programs such as Hard Copy or Inside Edition. An example is WSVN-TV, the Fox station in Miami. With an emphasis on spot news, high-energy anchors, and dramatic writing, this station is controversial but successful.

Alternative formats. Some stations have experimented with different ways to serve the different needs of the news audience. WCCO-TV, the CBS-owned station in Minneapolis, is splitting its late newscast in two, using a UHF channel. On the UHF station, WCCO offers alternative coverage to the station's regular VHF channel 4. Both stations carry the same first news block, but then mix coverage. For instance, the UHF station stays with news while the VHF channel does sports. Other stations have alternative early newscasts on cable or public stations. These stations are trying to find ways to reach a fragmenting audience. The long-term implications of these experiments are important because stations and cable operations may be able to broadcast alternative content at the same time, using different channels in digital television. Such broadcasts are some time away, but you need to keep up with developments in digital television because you will be affected.

Consultants

Leading and fueling much of this change in local news are news consultants. At one time consultants were seen as evil people who could cost you your job. Frankly, consultants were feared because they brought the bad news that stations were producing boring newscasts.

In fact, the consultants drove most of the changes in local and even network news. These firms, like Frank N. Magid, McHugh and Hoffman, and Audience Research & Development, all have backgrounds in market research. They understood how to ask the viewers the right kinds of questions, and helped stations meet the needs of their viewers.

Change is difficult, and critics and displaced anchors attacked the consultants. They blamed the consultants when stations tried the happy talk format and did so badly. They said the consultants put entertainment ahead of journalism.

In Chapter 14, you'll learn about the market research consultants do for stations. That research is extremely valuable when you are trying to find out what kind of news the audience wants and needs from your newscast.

As you know, the devil is in the details. Next, you'll look those devilish details in the eyes, and examine the mechanics of putting a newscast together. It's a daunting task at first, but the quicker you can master the mechanics of producing, the sooner you can become a power producer.

Chapter 8

Role Three: Production Expert

The Devil Is in the Details

In This Chapter:

- The News Hole
- The Rundown
- Back-timing Tips
- Scripts
- Paperwork or Production Orders

Chapter 8:
The Devil Is in the Details

"A good rundown shows every element you plan to put in the broadcast and where it goes."

t's one of the most horrible moments you face as a newscast producer. As the anchor reads the tease before the last break you look at the clock and then at your computer. Somehow you are 45 seconds over, or heavy. Up until this moment your back-timing had been perfect. You quickly recheck the rundown and the back-timing to make sure you haven't missed something. No luck. There's no way you're going to get this newscast off on time unless you act quickly. So you let everyone know the show is in trouble and then you start dropping pages. You're forced to kill the heavily teased kicker story, a major sin, and then you tell the anchors in their earpieces to just say a quick goodnight. With luck, you didn't upcut, or run over, into the next program. The end of the newscast is a jumble.

What happened? You missed a detail. Maybe you failed to enter a time in the proper rundown column, or the sportscaster ran over because he added late scores. All sorts of different problems can ruin a newscast, but power producers master the details to prevent such disasters.

For a beginning producer, the details, or the mechanics of producing, look daunting. Unfortunately, some producers never make it past this stage. These producers constantly worry about the details of production and forget about the real job of creating a newscast that people want to watch. However, there is no need for you to stall out at this point in your career. You can pick up producing mechanics in a few days, particularly if you take time to learn the newsroom computer and production systems. It's not hard. However, failing to command the minutiae of newscast production means you'll never be a successful producer.

In this chapter you'll learn how to master these details, to calculate the news hole, to construct a rundown, and learn the intricacies of back-timing. Finally, you'll discover scripting, organizing your rundown, and the paperwork of producing.

The News Hole

The starting point for putting together a broadcast is knowing how much time you have for news, sports and weather. To find this time, you calculate the news hole. This is the amount of time in the newscast for actual news content. Television news time isn't flexible unless you have a major crisis and can preempt scheduled programming. You have a set amount of time.

Knowing your news hole makes you a more decisive producer. Calculating your news hole helps you decide what stories to include in the broadcast and how long each story deserves to run. The time allowed by the news hole also helps you decide how stories should be produced. For example, should it be a voice-over or do you have enough time for a reporter's package? This helps you and the production team get organized.

The log. Each day the station's traffic department issues and distributes a printed computer log for the next day. This log shows every program, every public service announcement, every commercial, and every FCC-required station identification or ID. The log includes the timings for your broadcast and commercials, station promotions and pre-show teases. They're all timed to the second.

Generally, your on and

TIP
COMMERCIAL CONFLICT

One important reason to review the log every day is to spot commercials that conflict with certain news stories. You wouldn't want to run a train wreck story just before an Amtrak commercial. When you see a conflict, get in touch with the sales or traffic departments immediately, and ask them to move the commercial. Remember that it takes time to change commercials already programmed by computer for playback.

off times for the news broadcast are the same each day. The newscast will carry a set number of commercials. Even when sales are slow the traffic department may fill these commercial slots with public service announcements (PSAs), or commercials for the station, called promos. This keeps your news hole consistent.

If you think you might be able to use some of the PSA or promotional time for news content, talk first to your executive producer and then the traffic department. Never drop a PSA or promo without first getting permission. Remember that promotional spots are an investment in your own station and public service announcements are a contribution to your community.

Calculating the news hole. This process is relatively easy but does require you to learn to subtract in minutes and seconds. It's also a unique skill you need in order to master back-timing. To determine the news hole, start by finding your out or off time in the log (see box, right). This is the exact second the newscast is over. This out time will read something like 6:28:57. This leaves enough time for commercials between the newscast and the next program. In this example you have two 30-second commercials and a 3-second station ID before the next program.

Commercials take most of your news time. Within any broadcast are commercial breaks, where spots are grouped together. But these don't always run the same length. Say your broadcast has four internal 2-minute-and-10-second breaks. With the popularity of 15- and 10-second commercials, you do get breaks that run different lengths. In addition, because local news is popular with advertisers, many stations sell 10-second commercial billboards. The sales department likes to sell billboards for sports, weather or anything else advertisers want. Depending on the sponsor's advertising campaign, billboards might not run every night.

At this point in calculating your news hole, you have 8 minutes and 40 seconds of commercials inside your program. Subtract the commercials from 6:28:57 and you now have 20:17 left. The number of commercial breaks, four in this example, determines the number of blocks to the broadcast. So in this case you have five.

This scenario presumes the newscast starts precisely at 6 p.m., which is not typical. Depending on the format, you may have 15 or 20 seconds of

CALCULATING YOUR NEWS HOLE

Off time	6:28:57
Commercials	8:40
Weather	2:30
Sports	3:00
Tosses	:30
Teases	1:00
Open	:10
Close/Credits	:30
News Hole	12:37

pre-show teases immediately after the lead-in program. After this pre-show tease, you may run a couple of commercials, but smart stations omit these commercials so they can start the newscast before their competition. In this era of the remote control and impatient viewers, you can gain an advantage. These commercials are incorporated within the newscast so the station doesn't lose money.

Now subtract the other regular parts of the newscast, such as the taped open and the teases before each commercial break. Then subtract sports and weather, plus time for the anchor toss before and after both segments. Depending on their relative importance, sports and weather vary in time and placement. In a 30-minute newscast they should run from 6 to 7 minutes, including crosstalk.

Some stations still run closing credits and music at the end of the program. This can take another 15 seconds. Most stations still airing credits try to save time and run them as lower-third supers while the anchors sign off.

A regularly scheduled franchise segment also cuts into your news time. But don't cut a franchise. During ratings periods, you'll also find your news hole further reduced by special reports. Like franchises, these reports are heavily promoted and can't be cut from the broadcast unless authorized by the news director.

The Rundown

Now that you know how much time you have, your next step is to create your rundown. It's your

TIP
WALL RUNDOWNS

News people often laugh about the bad communication in newsrooms. Some stations producing an hour or more of news in the evening try to improve communications with the production team by writing the rundown on a large, wall-size, dry erase board, visible throughout the newsroom. When there is a change in the rundown it can be communicated on the wall board using a different colored marker. It works.

basic tool. It's how you communicate your plan to your news team. A good rundown shows every element you plan to put in the broadcast and where it goes. It's the road map of your newscast.

In all but the smallest newsrooms the rundown is a computer-generated format. This is handy because it allows you to create a tentative rundown early and then make changes as the day progresses. You can also experiment with different line-ups to see how a certain story flow might work. Most importantly, the computer allows you to add new stories easily even while your newscast is on the air.

As a producer, you absolutely must master the intricacies of the rundown. The rundown must be complete in every detail if you want to see your ideas and plans successfully executed. Leaving out the most seemingly minor detail can cause a first-class on-air disaster.

Standard rundowns. Over the years, television newsrooms have developed a fairly uniform approach to rundowns. The important information always goes in the same place on the rundown so everyone knows exactly where to look. Each of the popular newsroom computer systems has a standard rundown template based on this uniform approach. However, because each station seems to have minor variations on the basic format, computer systems are designed so newsrooms can easily change the rundown template.

Distribution of the rundown is key to a clean newscast. Get your plan out to everyone involved in the production of the newscast, from anchors, reporters, tape editors and writers, to the director, TD, audio person and tape playback person. While it may look like overkill, it's safer to distribute too many copies.

This rundown, which comes from the AP Newscenter software program, is for a single anchor late newscast. AP Newscenter prints out different formats for different positions. The columns don't match the order outlined here but can be altered to meet your personal preference.

Rundown columns. As you can see in the illustration, the printed rundown is in columns (see box, right). Each column is labeled at the top starting on the left with the page number, story slug, anchors, timing and tape treatment.

Not every newsroom follows this same column order. There are variations on this plan. Just be sure that all of these columns are included or the rundown won't serve its purpose.

To avoid confusion and to help communications, standardize the abbreviations on rundowns. Actually, the better computer programs have standard video and audio abbreviations that can be inserted with a single keystroke, a macro, or from a pull-down menu.

What follows is the most common way of arranging the columns in a rundown, and seems to be the most logical, despite what AP may use for its default rundown.

Page numbers. Because page numbers are extremely important both during the production process and during the newscast, most rundowns have the numbers on the outside left column. Page numbers are important because you normally use the number instead of the story slug when making changes. For instance, when you add a story or kill a story while you are on the air, always refer to the page number, not the slug.

Late script numbers. The best system for adding stories late in the process, after the script has been printed, is to give the new story a number such as "Pre1." This tells everyone that this story will run before the first story in the show. In other words, it's a new lead story. Pre22 would run after story 21 in the second block, and before story number 22.

Anchor assignments. In the second column you place initials for the anchors or reporters who appear live in the newscast. Use the same initials for the same

TIP
STANDARD RUNDOWN FORMAT

Creating your own version of the rundown, different from the station's other newscasts, can be a problem. Every rundown should conform to a station standard so that, for instance, a director assigned to another show could easily step in and direct your broadcast.

Eleven at 11 — **Producer Rundown**

Date: Thursday, May 06, 1999 Time: 11:00:00 PM Out Time: 11:32:20 PM

Page	Story/Slug	OnCam	Length	Timing	Camera	Effects	Type	Writer
A00.1	PREHEAD-1	Rod	00:00	11:00:00 PM			VO	
A00.2	PREHEAD-2							
A00.3	PREHEAD-3							
A01	CLOPEN-1	Rod						
A02	SHOW OPEN							
A03	==	Rod						
A04	ROBBER LIVE							
A05	ROBBER PKG							
A06	ROB TAG							
A07	POWERS	Rod						
A08	DIVERS	Rod						
A09	SU RIOT IN	Rod						
A10	SU RIOT LIVE							
A11	SU RIOT PKG							
A12	SU TAG	Rod						
A13	SEX OFFENDER	Rod; Rod						
A14	QUICK DRAW	Rod; Rod						
A15	GREEN FEE	Rod						
A16	SLEPIAN	Rod						
A17	REFUGEES	Rod						
A18	1ST WEATHER							
A19	1ST SPORTS	Doug						
A20	TSE A-1 HEALTH	Rod						
A21	TSE A-2 CNYMUSIC							
A22	TSE A-3 TULIPS							
B00	--- BREAK 1 ---							
B01	BUMP IN							
B02	TULIP FEST	Rod						
B03	CROW ATTACKS	Rod						
B04	JOHNY VEGAS	Rod						
B05	JOHNY VEGAS PKG							
B06	JOHNY VEGAS TAG	Rod						
B07	WEATHER							
B08	TSE B-1 SPORTS	Rod						
B09	TSE B-2 MONEY			11:19:02 PM			VO	
B10	PRIZE PATROL		00:30	11:18:55 PM			SOT	
C00	--- BREAK 2 ---		02:46	11:19:38 PM		=========		
C01	BUMPBACK			11:22:24 PM			BETACART	
C02	ATT-MICROSOFT	Rod	00:23	11:22:11 PM		TAKE VO	TAPE TOP	
C03	STOX	Rod	00:14	11:22:36 PM	1 SHOT	TAKE VO	TAPE TOP	
C04	HEALTHCAST	Rod	01:37	11:22:52 PM	1 SHOT	TAKE PKG	SOT	
C05	TSE C-1 SPORTS	Rod	00:25	11:24:32 PM	1 SHOT	TAKE VO	VO	
C06	LOTTERY			11:24:57 PM			CHYRON/S	
D00	--- BREAK 3 ---		02:41	11:24:51 PM		=========		
D01	SPORTSNIGHT OPEN		03:40	11:27:32 PM		TAKE VO	VO	
D02	SABRES/BRUINS	Doug		11:31:12 PM		TAKE VO :00	VO	
D03	NHL BOARD			11:31:12 PM			CHYRON/S	
D04	SKYCHIEFS	Doug		11:31:12 PM			ON CAMER	
D05	YANKS/TWINS			11:31:12 PM		TAKE VO	VO	
D06	BASEBALL BOARD			11:31:12 PM			CHYRON/S	
D07	DIRT/DALE PLANK	Doug		11:31:12 PM		TAKE VO :00 TAKE SOT :08 TAKE VO :34	VO/SOT	
D08	ABC BOWLING			11:31:12 PM		TAKE VO TAKE SOT :10 TAKE VO :28	VO/SOT	
D09	VERNON	Doug		11:31:12 PM		TAKE VO	VO	
D10	VERNON BOARD			11:31:12 PM			CHYRON/S	
D11	ELSEWHERE	Doug		11:31:12 PM			ON CAMER	
D12	SPORTS 10			11:31:12 PM				
D13	SPORTS 11			11:31:12 PM				
D14	SPORTS12			11:31:12 PM				
D15	SPORTS13			11:31:12 PM				
D16	SPORTS14			11:31:12 PM				
D17	SPORTS15			11:31:12 PM				
D18	TOSSBACK		00:10	11:31:12 PM			ON CAMER	
D19	JOHNY VEGAS SOT	Rod	01:00	11:31:22 PM		TAKE VO TAKE SOT	SOT	

Courtesy WIXT-TV

anchor for each and every broadcast. Some rundowns put the anchor names in the third column after the story slug, but it's easier in the control room to have the names in the column between the page number and the story slug. When anchors appear in a two-shot, both are on camera at the same time, so put both initials separated by a slash. That will tell the director and camera operators that you plan a two-shot. Do the same when an anchor is tossing to weather or sports. When both anchors do the lead-in to a package or live report, then use separate pages for each anchor's part of the lead-in, separately numbered, so the director and the anchors are clear about what you plan.

Story slug. Each story in your lineup has a name, known as a story slug. A slug is a simple one- or two-word description of a story. For example, "Supt. Quits," "School Layoff," "GE Strike," or "Downtown Murder." Make sure the assignment editor uses the same story slug on the assignment list and on the assignment board.

Graphics. This fourth column should be used to indicate which graphic from the still store you intend to use over the anchor's shoulder. This over-the-shoulder box is intended to help the audience easily understand what the story is about. Most newsrooms indicate a slug for the graphic in this column or use the still store number that's used to recall the graphic. Don't be surprised if the newsroom uses the name of the machine used as the source of the visual. This leads to all kinds of different labels such as Adda or Quantel, brands of still store systems. This column is also where you can indicate a reporter or interview subject being placed in a video box next to the anchor. This is called dueling boxes, a good way to place the anchor with reporters or interview subjects when they are at a remote location.

Tape/Video. The fifth column of the rundown is for the video treatment. This designates the way videotape is used in each story. Your rundown will show just how the tape is being used, such as a reporter package (PKG), or an anchor voice-over (VO), or a voice-over to sound bite (VOSOT). If there isn't any video for a story, such as a reader or copy story, you normally leave a blank space.

PKG or VOSOT or VO are the most common ways of designating tape usage, but video abbreviations can differ. For some stations it all depends on the nomenclature the newsroom used when first making the transition from film to tape. Because tape and film were used in the same broadcast, the producers would have to be clear about the source. This means you still see abbreviations like "ejpkg" or "engpkg" or "vtrvo," which continue in use despite the absence of film.

You also may hear terms such as "anchor package" for a pre-recorded voice-over by one of the anchors. In fact, there are almost as many different terms as there are newsrooms!

The video column also is where you indicate a microwave live shot or satellite live report. You use this column to indicate a report from the newsroom camera, known as the flash camera, or other video sources such as a towercam. Each station also has different abbreviations for these video sources. Just be consistent and specific.

Time. The story length goes in the next column. At first, in your preliminary rundown, you put in an approximate time for each story. As you prepare your newscast, round off story length to the nearest 5 seconds, unless you already have the precise time.

As each story is completed, put the exact time into your computer rundown. Make sure this actual time is the time used by the computer for back-timing.

Read rate. Something else to consider in the time of each story is your anchor's read rate. This is the number of words an anchor reads aloud in a minute. Each anchor's read rate can be programmed into the computer, but this is not perfect. Power producers check this time by having the anchor read aloud as they time the story using a stopwatch.

Story length. The length of each story is critical to the pace and flow of your newscast. Negotiating story length with reporters is one of the most demanding aspects of your job. You can't afford to have a story run too long or too short. At the same time, you don't want to prevent a reporter from doing a good story. Negotiating story length takes good questions, an open mind and an understanding of story structure. As the editors finish the reporters' tape packages, they should give you the exact running time of the tape. It is not unusual to go on the air with a piece still being edited. Before air, make sure you have a realistic time for the story so you're not surprised!

Back-timing Tips

The final column on the rundown is for back-timing. This column shows the countdown, by the second, to the exact time your broadcast must be off the air. Thanks to the use of computers and printed rundowns, back-timing isn't as difficult as it used to be. Computers are accurate and quick as long as the times that go into

---

TIP: CONSISTENT SLUGS

When someone arbitrarily changes a story slug in the middle of the process, you stand a good chance of having a mistake. For instance, a tape goes back to tape playback labeled "Weston Out," instead of the proper slug, "Supt. Quits." The playback person is in a tough spot. The rundown or tape list will say "Supt. Quits." If the playback person knows Weston is superintendent of schools it might be all right, but if he has to ask you or someone else where to run the tape, then there can be problems.

TIP: LAST-MINUTE SAVES

If a tape's time is seriously off as you are getting ready to start your newscast, enlist another producer or the EP to get the story back down to something approaching the negotiated time. They can save you from having to drop the story and destroying the flow and pace of the broadcast.

your back-timing are correct.

Actually, having to do the subtraction yourself, without a calculator, is a great discipline. It lets you do a quick calculation in your head when up against a deadline with no computer or calculator. Also, never trust the computer to keep you on time. It's up to you to check times like tape length and to keep your live reports to the allotted time.

Controlling the timing on air is perhaps the most challenging technical part of producing. You must make some tough decisions while the broadcast moves along. You want to maintain the flow and pace, give your anchors time to react to stories, and to keep the production looking smooth to the viewers. Here are some ways you can take command of back-timing.

■ When you go on the air, your broadcast should be light by 20 or 30 seconds. Unexpected events, like late roll cues or a gabby weathercaster, eat up time quickly.

■ The final anchor sign-off and tease to the next newscast should be done with comfort and authority. Back-time to the start of these final pages. This makes your anchors look good.

Interview: Newscast Director

Phil Hutchings
Newscast Director
WDIV-TV
Detroit

Phil Hutchings directs newscasts for WDIV, the NBC affiliate in Detroit. He graduated from Syracuse University in 1978 and began directing in Bangor, ME. Phil moved on to Binghamton, NY, and then Rochester, NY, before joining WDIV as a newscast director. He has also been a production manager in Miami, a program director in Birmingham, AL, and a freelance director.

What is an ideal relationship between a producer and director?

It's a partnership based on trust. I use a pilot/flight controller analogy. The director is much like the pilot and the producer is the flight controller. When the flight controller tells you to come down a few thousand feet, you come down. But, if the plane—or in our case, the newscast—is going to hit the top of a mountain, you need to let the controller know.

Trust is the key to making the relationship between producer and director work. Producers accept it when I say I can't do something and we go from there. However, a director should try to avoid saying no, should always try to make an idea work.

Why does that relationship break down? And when does it break down?

The breakdowns I have seen are when producers don't understand the production process. An ownership issue over the newscast can create problems, too.

Producers create programs, but at some point they have to hand it over to the director and trust him or her with it. There are times when I get the feeling producers may consider the program *theirs*—it should be thought of as *ours*. When you start hearing this is "my program" or "my area," that's a caution flag. Producers I've enjoyed working with have considered the program a team effort. They ask, "What do you think of this or how did that work?"

The trust factor comes with time and experience by working together. I learn to trust when I know the producer understands the limitations I face in the control room. And on the other hand, the director has to under-

- Make sure the anchors have enough pad copy, two minutes at least, so that they don't have to make inane blather if you are short. It makes the audience uncomfortable and sends them to the remote control.
- Don't always rely on weather to cut or add time. Weather is always near the top of the list when it comes to what the audience wants from your newscast, so give weather enough time. Don't cheat your audience.
- When dropping a story or adding copy, communicate clearly and decisively. Leave enough time to get the word to everyone who will have to drop or add pages. Try to make page changes during a break. After you make a change, check with your anchors and directors to be certain they have the correct page order for the next block.
- Always use page numbers when making a change. There's a strong chance someone will misunderstand if you use a story slug.
- Don't ever yell into the anchors' earpieces while they are reading copy. You only make it difficult for them to read the copy. Communicate changes only during commercials or packages. Use

stand what the producer is going through in stacking the show and putting it all together in terms of journalism.

The working relationship between a producer and a director is so critical. It's a marriage. And they both need to understand each other and respect each other.

What are some of the things the producer does that makes your job more difficult?

Pushing the envelope too far. It's great to try to do something better. If you can lift 450 pounds and you are trying to lift 460 pounds, you may get it. However, don't try to go to 500 pounds too quickly. I know a terrific producer who's overly ambitious. He doesn't ask about our capability. In his mind he conceives a wonderful show and feels we should be able to execute all the production elements. He needs to involve the director in his planning for it to become reality.

Don't settle for a turnkey-style director, who expects everything to be done for them. They arrive in the newsroom and ask where the script and rundowns are. Give them things to do such as the pre-production graphics that get done in the control room. If possible, have them attend the afternoon meeting; you'll never regret it. Create a pride of ownership.

What are some of the things newscast directors do that get in the way of a positive working relationship?

Some directors make jokes about the show and news product. I heard about a director who used to carry a bell into the control room and every time there was a mistake he felt was the producer's he would ring the bell. That's a horrible joke. It just drives the two apart.

Producers and directors have to remember who the competition is. While there's a natural competition between a producer and a director, at some point you have to remind each other what the real competition is. It's not between producer and director. It's the other stations in town.

What are some tips you would give new producers? What should they do to learn about the production process?

Spend as much time in the control room as possible. Try to understand how things work. Learn the communication system. Frustrations comes when a production team is trying to do something and they feel the producer doesn't understand what is going on and doesn't care.

During the newscast, producers need to treat the director just as they do talent. When an anchor stumbles, a producer wouldn't get on the IFB and say to the anchors, "What the hell did you say that for? You blew that line." At least they shouldn't because it would shatter the anchor. But producers sometimes treat directors will less respect and consideration. I've had producers slam phones and start yelling and screaming when something went wrong. This can derail a director. Producers need to say, "Get on with it, go forward." Conversely, the turning point to being a successful director is when you make a mistake and just turn the script page over and move on. The times I've picked up a script page that's already aired to see what I did wrong, five or six more bad things happen. Don't look back until the show is over.

How can producers

the intercom telephone instead of the earpiece.

Scripts

Once you've completed and distributed the rundown, you then turn to the script. Hopefully, much of the script is already written. In the time leading up to the newscast, your job is to make sure the script is edited and assembled properly.

Make sure they're consistent. Each script should be done in the same format for each newscast. Fortunately, the widespread use of computers with their built-in script formats and video commands makes scripting more uniform. It's now a matter of filling in the blanks on the screen from a pull-down menu. Still, the story slug and everything else on the script must conform to your rundown.

For television production your script format is set up with margins on the right side of the page for writing your story. All the video, graphics, timing, and production information go on the left side of the script where it won't be seen by the anchors when they are reading off the prompter. Windows-based software packages have script

---

learn more about production and the people on the production team? Many producers don't have much contact with the production team until they hit the control room.

They need to realize it's not their full-time office. During the news they are like a guest in the control room for 30 or 60 minutes. Directors and the production crew work in the control room and studio all day. Producers need to say, "This is an area I'm not in for a large part of the day but I'm in there for a critical part of that day. I have to take the time to go in and introduce myself, ask questions."

They have to literally look right at the people and say, "I am here to get a better understanding for what you guys do and what information I can provide for you." Be upfront with them to make your job easier. Realize that the control room is the production staff's area of expertise. Also understand they see producers come and go all the time. In some stations it's hard to remember the names of the producers. They're not there long enough.

New producers have to remember that newsroom relationships are built over time. There is a period that the new person won't have the shared history that makes up the station and newsroom cultures. Take your time to fit in. Don't come in and say, "In my last job we used to do it this way, or in my old station we did it this way." People won't be impressed.

What else do producers do that gets in the way?

Not sharing information is perhaps the biggest problem. The director needs to know if you change something. The last thing the director wants to hear is, "Oh, I meant to tell you I dropped that."

What advice would you have for producers and directors in smaller markets?

Try lots of things. Just enjoy it. I don't do anything any differently when there are 15,000 households watching us versus 150,000 households. I do the show with the same intensity. It is really done for the 15 people working on the show. It is almost like a game we play every day and we have fun doing it.

Are there any more points you feel are important for beginning producers to know?

Learn how to remain calm in a control room and communicate clearly. I made a sign back in 1983. I grabbed a piece of paper out of one of the reporter pads. And I wrote "Mr. Calm" on it and I carried it into the control room with me for about two years. I put it right in front of me. I literally would look at that sign during a newscast if I got going too fast, too hot, or too angry. I still have it. Remain in control. That goes for producers, too.

It's important for producers to pay attention in the control room and not bury their head in the computer. Remember what is on the air is not always what's in the computer. If you can look three or four stories ahead, then your director needs to be two or three stories ahead. The technical director needs to be watching the air. Pay attention to what is happening in the control room and on all those monitors.

format macros to use.

Follow the anchor's lead. There's a debate in newsrooms over using upper or lower case in scripts. Actually, the best course is to follow newsroom and anchor requirements when typing copy. Some anchors like all upper case while others are more comfortable with upper and lower case. Find out what your anchors want in copy format.

Don't forget your grammar. The use of computers for word processing doesn't reduce the potential for copy errors, even if you use the spellchecker. Computers just make it easier to correct errors. Bad grammar and misspelled words can cause your anchor to stumble or look bad. So be sure to check your copy.

Make multiple copies. Computer printers produce multiple copies a good deal easier to read than the old script books. However, most newsrooms still assign colored scripts by job. In most newsrooms your production assistant or desk assistant will assemble the script and distribute it to the right people.

If a script is not completed in time for the director to mark, the producer creates a numbered dummy page with video and graphics information. This page tells the director what production elements will be in this story even though there's no complete script, so he or she can plan camera moves, tape playback, and graphics.

Paperwork or Production Orders

Along with the rundown, the production staff needs several production orders and lists. These lists flow directly from the rundown and are generated by your computer system.

Tape list. Tape playback will need a list of each videotape to play during the news. This list is done by story slug, or tape number, or both. This is one reason story slugs are so important.

Super or CG list. The character generator operator will need a list of all the supers to be used on air in their proper order and with the number to recall them.

Graphics list: This is a list of all the graphics on the rundown that are accessed from the still store computer. It should include a story slug and the number used to recall the graphic.

Graphics order form. It is good practice to have regular order forms for graphics to give the artist so it's clear what the graphic is all about. Share them with the director and the reporter if the graphic goes inside the reporter's story, particularly if the graphic is going to be created during pre-production.

As you can see, mastering the news production process looks formidable. However, as you gain confidence and experience, you grow past the mechanic phase of producing. Once you've mastered the details of the production process, it's time to face three important segments of your newscast: weather, sports and franchises. Power producers know skillful handling of these three elements can help win viewers, and do wonders for their careers.

TIP: EDITORIAL CONTROL

Your newsroom computer network can be set up so that all scripts must be approved before they can be printed. The best system is to have the news director, executive producer or managing editor review and approve the copy for accuracy, legal problems, and style before sending it on to be printed. This provides a level of editorial control often missing in television newsrooms.

POWER PRODUCER CHECKLIST

This checklist is designed to help you organize your work flow during the news day. At some point you need to accomplish each of these tasks to prepare your newscast.

Before Work
- ❏ Arrive early and prepared.
- ❏ Have you read all the newspapers and listened to the radio newscasts?
- ❏ Did you watch the station's latest newscast and the competition's newscasts?
- ❏ Keep a list of potential stories from the newspapers and newscasts for the story meeting.

Eight to Nine Hours before Newscast
- ❏ Prepare for story meeting.
- ❏ Read wires.
- ❏ Check in with assignment desk.
- ❏ Check feed rundowns. List potential stories.

Seven Hours
- ❏ Story meeting.
- ❏ Do you have a potential lead story?
- ❏ Do you have a potential kicker?
- ❏ What is the status of any special reports or franchise stories planned for your broadcast?

Six Hours
- ❏ Check on potential live shots and order satellite time if needed.
- ❏ Talk to reporters and photographers about the "focus" of their stories before they go out.
- ❏ Start preliminary program rundown.
- ❏ Prepare first draft of graphics and pre-production needs based on story meeting and reporter conversations.
- ❏ Assign copy to writers. Discuss graphics and video.
- ❏ Draft teases.
- ❏ See if current show producer needs help.

Four to Five Hours
- ❏ Start CG/super process.
- ❏ Check on network and syndicated feeds.
- ❏ Finish preliminary rundown.

Three to Four Hours
- ❏ Run show meeting.
- ❏ Distribute final approved rundown.
- ❏ Finish ordering graphics and discuss pre-production with artists and directors.
- ❏ Order live shots.

Two Hours
- ❏ Check on tape editing.
- ❏ Start editing copy and scripts.
- ❏ Check for transition lines.
- ❏ Review all reporter scripts including franchises.

One Hour
- ❏ Write final teases based on final stories.
- ❏ Check and reconfirm live shots, particularly satellite.
- ❏ Check on tape editing.
- ❏ Print script.
- ❏ Distribute script.

30 Minutes
- ❏ Final check on tape editing. Discuss any problem stories and decide on contingencies.
- ❏ Review final rundown with director and discuss any contingencies.
- ❏ Double-check supers and graphics.
- ❏ Tapes to playback.
- ❏ Last check of wires and with assignment desk just before air.
- ❏ Check IFBs, radios and live shots.

Post Show
- ❏ Debrief with anchors and production crew after show.
- ❏ Review and solve any problems.
- ❏ Write note to next show producer on any opportunities or problems he or she needs to know about for the next broadcast.
- ❏ Give assignment desk any story ideas.
- ❏ Check on status of any franchises or special reports planned for your broadcast tomorrow.

Note: Use this list as the basis for your own checklist. Put backtimes on the key tasks you need to complete for your news broadcast.

Chapter 9

Role Three: Production Expert

More Than News

In This Chapter:

- Weather
- Weather Emergencies
- Sports
- Franchises
- Sweeps
- Live Reports
- Interviews

Chapter 9: More Than News

> "You can't afford to ignore sports or any other part of your newscast."

For the entire news day you've been struggling to develop a strong lead for your newscast. Your options are weak: a new director for the county library or a wrongful death lawsuit in a case no viewer will remember. As you and your colleagues struggle with this dilemma in the afternoon story meeting, the sportscaster comes in and says he needs a crew to go over to the local university. The assignment editor responds that all the photographers are assigned. As an afterthought he asks why sports needs a crew this late. "Can't you guys plan better?" The sportscaster says this might be important. He's just heard the school is being placed on NCAA probation for recruiting violations. Suddenly, you have a lead story.

Of course, it's not every day that a sports story leads a newscast, but it happens. This is a good reason why you can't afford to ignore sports or any other part of your newscast.

Power producers understand a newscast has more than hard news, and they work to make every section interesting and pertinent. This applies to sports, weather, franchises, live reports and interviews. In this chapter you'll learn how you make these newscast elements contribute to a winning newscast. You'll find the tools you need to make these segments into something viewers want to watch. And you'll gain valuable ideas to make live reports and interviews more entertaining.

Weather

Weather is the most important part of your newscast. In research surveys the audience ranks weather at the top as the most important news element. This certainly makes sense when you think about the impact of weather on your audience; it touches everyone. Viewers want to know how to dress the children for school and if they can plan on a picnic outdoors.

Weather is a critical factor in a successful newscast. In market after market you find stations where weather coverage and weather personalities make the difference when it comes to ratings. This is another reason why you've got to pay close attention to weather.

Fair weather friends. Even if you realize the importance of weather, communication between you and the weather staff is frequently difficult. Weather people and producers often clash for two reasons.

For one thing, weathercasters generally work someplace other than the newsroom. If they don't have their own office, they work off the news set. That's often where their computers are located. This physical separation makes it difficult for you to communicate easily with your weathercaster. You have to make it a point to talk to the weathercaster frequently during the news day. Clear communication is critical because you need to know what is going on in the weather. You need to know today's weather story in order to write teases and if warranted, to turn weather into a major story. You also need to anticipate future weather because it can become a major story, and a day or two of warning makes all the difference when it comes to winning coverage.

On top of the physical separation, you strain relations with the weather staff when you cut back the weather block to get the newscast back on time. This drives weathercasters nuts. After all, they're passionate about weather. Also, cutting weather is a disservice to the audience. Why cut the most important information in the newscast?

Above all, build a relationship of mutual respect with your weather staff. If you're forced to cut weather, give them plenty of warning. However, your first option should be to cut news or sports, not weather. Communicate clearly any time you make a change in the way they produce the weather block.

Make the weather understandable. Since

TIP
METEOROLOGIST OR WEATHERCASTER

A source of newsroom debate and teeth gnashing is whether or not to call your weathercaster a meteorologist. Since the title adds credibility to the forecast, news directors like it, but those on-air meteorologists who have degrees in the subject get furious when someone without proper qualifications calls himself a meteorologist. The rule is to use the title only when your weather person has a meteorology degree or the American Meteorological Society's seal, which requires advanced training.

---

weather is frequently the big news story of the day, work with the weathercaster to present it properly. Remember that many weather people are trained as meteorologists and don't have reporting experience. It's your job to work with them to orchestrate their use of video, create additional maps to help tell the story, and to review their script.

One of the problems in using weathercasters as reporters is their use of technical jargon. They use words that sound important like "precipitation" instead of rain or snow, and phrases like "tornadic activity." They of course also use real technical terms from meteorology that aren't easily understood. You need to help them make their weather report understandable. Also, keep weather jargon out of your teases and tosses.

Weather Emergencies

A weather emergency is news, significant news. Hurricanes, blizzards, ice storms, tornadoes and flooding are major news events for you and your station. These events can take lives and cause huge damage to a community or region. In fact, because weather emergencies touch everyone in a market, these stories are the most important news stories for your viewers. Owning a major weather story is a challenge, but also an opportunity.

Community lifeline. Emergency weather is more than a chance to show off your Super Doppler 5000 radar or your PinPoint Weather Tracker. When severe weather hits, your station provides a major service to the community. People turn to their local stations for the latest information on what is happening and what might happen. They need information on how to cope with the disaster. For instance, they need to know where to go to find shelter and emergency supplies. Afterwards, they also need help on cleaning up and emergency aid.

As you learned in Chapter 4, you and the rest of the newsroom need to go all out covering a weather emergency. Your newsroom will go on the air and try to stay on the air to help the community. That should be part of your newsroom's plan for disaster coverage. Even with a good disaster plan, you will have to use all of your producing skills and creativity to help the station meet its commitment.

The payoff. In more than one case, stations have done such a great job in covering a weather disaster or emergency that they have won loyal viewers for decades. One case was WJXT-TV, the CBS affiliate in Jacksonville, FL. The weathercaster, George Winterling, did such a superb job of predicting where a hurricane was headed that he was credited with helping save thousands of lives. Even though Winterling is now retired, the station continues to dominate the local ratings, part of a legacy of great weather coverage.

Sports

At the opposite end of viewer interest from weather is sports. While virtually every viewer is interested in the weather, most aren't interested in sports. Audience research consistently reports the interest in sports is limited to less than a quarter of the viewers.

So why do local newscasts include long sports blocks that sometimes run longer than the weather? To be successful, your newscast needs sports fans in the audience. Sports viewers represent ratings. Also, advertisers are trying to reach the young sports viewers, men 18 to 49.

Jock-ularity. You face the same problem in communicating with sports as you do with weather. The sports department is usually in a corner of the newsroom or in a separate office, and sports

---

TIP
FOLLOW UP

Telling people that bad weather is headed their way is only part of your job. In the aftermath of a weather disaster your newsroom needs to go all out covering the cleanup. Look for stories such as price gouging, health problems, and how well prepared local disaster agencies were. You also need to reach out to victims through food, clothing and fund drives. There are countless ways, from telethons to community bulletin boards, that stations can serve their community during the aftermath.

reporters often have little interest in the rest of the news. Also, your sportscaster probably doesn't fully understand how he fits in the mix of news, weather and sports. You can help build rapport on set between the news anchors and sports. Brief the anchors on the big sports news of the day. And show the anchors' interest in sports by opening their microphones during sports and encouraging them to comment on interesting or funny video.

Frequently a sports story does command wide interest. In bigger markets there are sports producers to help you work with the sports staff. However, in medium and small markets, sportscasters still produce their own segments.

When a sports story is important enough to lead your show or go in the A block, produce that story with care and attention. If anything, producing a sports story as news is more difficult. You need to sell this story to non-sports fans so they understand its importance. You have to find a strong hook.

Producing sports for the non-fan. The best sportscasters make sports interesting to the non-fan. They pull in viewers who don't religiously watch ESPN. You can help by working with sports to tease the most interesting sports news or video, and by providing local sports story ideas. Keep a lookout for memorable sports video on the feeds.

Viewers want to see profiles of local sports people and coverage of local events more than they want the baseball box scores. Power producers give sports time to put these local sports stories together properly.

Franchises

Franchises are regularly scheduled reports on subjects that news research says are important to your viewers. Franchises are used as a promotional vehicle. Generally, the producer is told what it is going to be about, how much time to give it, and where to put the franchise in the broadcast.

Why do franchises? The answer is simple: franchises are a way to demonstrate that the station is covering the viewers' major concerns. If you look at a list of issues on the minds of the viewers, you'll find that franchises cover these major topics. At the top of this list are crime and medicine. Franchises also can target special audiences, like young parents or young males interested in technology. Franchises are merely another device for trying to serve the needs of the viewers.

Franchises are set aside in the newscast through special graphics, often animated with a music sting. They have titles such as "Eye on Health," "CrimeWatch" or "Consumer Alert." Also, most franchises are delivered by one of the anchors, live on set, which makes the franchise stand out from a standard reporter package. Franchises have to be on at a specific time in the newscast so they match the promotion.

Franchises vs. real reporting. Along with a lack of flexibility, producers also dislike franchises because they aren't timely news. Power producers understand this problem and work with the franchise reporters to make their stories newsworthy. A news hook makes the franchise more interesting and relevant to the viewers.

Make franchises local. The strongest franchises deal with local people and local issues. One of the most successful franchises is the "Action Line" or "On Your Side" consumer action franchise. Your local anchor solves consumer complaints for local people. Another strong local franchise is the "Crime Stopper" tip line in which local law-enforcement agencies present information about a local crime and ask for tips with a promise of a reward. These locally produced franchise reports take time and money; most medium- and small-market stations lack the resources to do local franchises.

Canned franchises. Many franchises are purchased from outside suppliers. While some are self-contained with a regular host on the tape, most purchased franchises come with a script. All your anchor has to do is record the narration. They aren't local and seldom timely. However, news directors like them because they are less expensive than a reporter and photographer doing a local story. However, they're generic and used all over the country. There are ways to get around the limitations of canned franchises. When fran-

---

TIP

PAY ATTENTION TO SPORTS

There are exceptions, but for some mysterious reason news producers often aren't interested in sports. Maybe they became producers because they were bad at sports as kids and spent their time watching local news. Whatever the reason, you need to approach learning about sports and keeping up on sports news just as you did in learning to be a journalist.

chises offer follow-up material like brochures, information sheets and recipes, localize this information with the names of nearby agencies that might be able to help with information. Offer this material at the end of the franchise. Then make sure your newsroom responds promptly when a viewer sends in for the material.

Phone banks. Another way to localize important issues is to invite viewers to call in questions to local experts. For instance, if you run a report on some medical problem, follow up by having doctors available to answer questions. Throughout the newscast, tease this phone bank. This idea can be applied to all kinds of different viewer concerns, from medicine to the law. You can arrange for the experts through local organizations like the bar association, a medical association or the Better Business Bureau.

Sweeps

During the four major Nielsen ratings sweeps months, your station needs to get people to watch your newscasts. Consequently, stations do series or special reports during sweeps to give the promotion department something specific and topical to advertise.

Sweeps series are frequently a source of friction between the news and promotion departments. News normally wants to do something newsworthy, while promotion likes stories they can promote easily. While the goals are the same, there's often conflict between the news department and the promotion department. You haven't been in television news long if you haven't heard a reporter blasting the promotion department over a promo he feels isn't in keeping with the basic theme of the series.

Special reports and series. News consultants provide stations promotable series ideas from other markets around the country. Not only do they supply tapes of the stories but they also can provide the promotional material. This leads to series or special reports that aren't local and are sensational for the sake of ratings. One recent example is the series on the cleanliness of hotel rooms where a local reporter would find all kinds of disgusting and filthy stains on the walls, carpet and bedding. The story was done by dozens of stations.

It's tough to find intriguing series that draw viewers, and aren't so dumb that viewers tune out. The solution to better special reports is long-term planning. News managers often overlook planning and this leads to major problems such as series that don't match the promotion or barely get done in time for air. You can force the issue by meeting with the executive producer, assignment editor and news director to start planning far in advance. This may not be in your job description, but if you don't, you'll get the stress when a special report is being edited against your deadline.

Sweeps ideas. When it comes to selecting topics, encourage everyone in the newsroom to come up with ideas. The more involvement from your team the better chance you have of coming up with a story about a local issue. Also, if a reporter or photographer suggests the idea and does the series, it's a strong morale boost. You also stand a chance of having a much better series because the person who suggested the topic will be interested in seeing that it's done well. Of course, a series also can be mandated by the general manager or news director or vetoed by the promotion department. Sweeps reports are so important virtually everyone in the station, for better or worse, gets their fingers in the effort.

Investigative reports. Investigative reporting is costly and time-consuming and hard to do well. Setting aside the time and people required to do a proper investigation is difficult, but you can often encourage investigative reporting as one way to make your sweeps series effective. In other words, sweeps are so important you can use Nielsen to justify the time and cost. Needless to say, this type of reporting takes extra attention and care on the part of the producer. You need to showcase it properly and be alert to legal and ethical issues.

TIP DIGESTS

 Like a franchise, the digest is delivered from the set and surrounded by special graphics and given a label. For example, the medical reporter will recap that day's top medical news, including local stories, and perhaps conduct a local interview. Some stations incorporate canned franchise material into a digest so the audience gets both local and national stories.

When it comes to special series or investigative reports, stations often assign producers to work with individual reporters to make sure all the production details are handled and that the project stays on track. For you, this can be an opportunity to explore a different side of producing and to get some field experience. The executive producer should develop a schedule for shooting, writing and editing these sweeps reports so they are finished before the promotion deadline. You should also work with the art department to develop appropriate graphics.

There has been a debate over the years about how effective long series are. Now, local news is moving away from long five- or three-part series and toward single special reports. Of course, the logistics are easier and the promotion department gets a wider variety of subjects to advertise.

Live Reports

Like franchises and special reports, audience research indicates that live reporting is something the audience finds valuable about local television news. Live reporting gives a sense of immediacy and excitement to any story because it looks like the station is on top of the latest news. Live reporting is something every station must do well.

Probably nothing has so revolutionized local television news in the last 20 years as ENG (electronic newsgathering) and SNG (satellite newsgathering). ENG and SNG provide instantaneous coverage, not only from your market but also from virtually anyplace in the world. The ability to go live to the scene of a story moved anchors and reporters out of the studio.

The live challenges. Live coverage presents enormous challenges. There are major ethical and legal issues involved, such as inadvertently showing a suicide or libeling someone during an ad-lib live report. You'll explore these issues later, but for you as a producer, dealing with live reporting every day presents a challenge.

In producing a live report, ask yourself if this live report is a good idea. Will it add to the newscast? Too many live reports are done purely

TIP
FOLLOW UP

Anytime you do a special report, series or investigative report, follow up on that report. Look for ways to provide additional information through brochures or your web site, and do additional stories later on new developments in the stories. Don't let the audience forget what you did for them.

for the sake of having a live reporter in a newscast. There are good reasons to report live from the scene: breaking spot news, a late development in a story, or to use a dramatic scene to introduce a special report.

When live reporting cheats or insults the viewers' intelligence, it's a tune-out. A common example is reporting live from the scene long after the event, when the location is devoid of people or interest. Avoid trite live shots such as reports from in front of a courthouse hours after a trial recessed, or in front of a darkened building long after a meeting concluded.

Planning, preparation and coordination. You create interesting live reporting through careful planning, adequate preparation of reporter and crew, and by effective coordination between location and studio. This may seem obvious, but it's often overlooked in newsrooms.

Before you decide to do a live report, make sure going live will enhance the story. Work with the assignment editors. Make sure the location makes sense, that something is actually happening, and that you can get a proper camera location. Too many times photographers and reporters are asked to go to a poorly chosen location that adds nothing to the story. For instance, it's hard to do a visually interesting live report on football training from a dark field three hours after practice ended. Another example would be a report on fall foliage from a mountaintop cloaked in fog.

Once it makes sense to send a crew, make sure reporters have the background information they need. There's no point in having reporters at the scene who don't know anything about the story. They need the latest information and the best possible background. It's a simple matter for you or the reporter to print out a search of the news wires or the Internet before they leave.

Also, before the reporter leaves, discuss what video is available and how she wants to use it. Ask questions. Will she want file video? Will she be editing in the truck and sending an edited story back or feeding raw video to be edited at the station? Does she plan a live interview? What about supers? Is the live report already scripted or will she be sending back a script? If there isn't time for a script, will she be able to get you enough script to have proper roll cues for the director? Cover as many of these details as you can before the crew leaves.

The next step in producing a live report is careful coordination. Let engineering know what to expect. If you are using the satellite truck, then engineering needs the satellite transponder coordinates. If it is a microwave shot, provide the channel and truck location. Also crucial for engineering are the times for the various live shots and where you plan to use them in your show. The producer is responsible for coordinating the live field report within the newscast. The producer tells the reporter whom to toss to for the next report or which anchor to address when tossing back to the studio. A reporter doing a live shot looks inept when the producer doesn't communicate the details. With cell phones, two-way radios and pagers, you can talk directly to the team in the field; make sure you do.

During a newscast, the producer communicates with the remote location using an internal system called an IFB (interruptible feedback.) The reporter and photographer hear you in their earpieces. It's up to you to give them proper countdowns and keep them informed during the newscast. At the same time, constant chatter can be distracting. It destroys concentration.

The Sony sandwich. The use of a tape in the middle of a live report is called a Sony sandwich or donut. This is because a piece of Sony videotape is the meat between the reporter's live introduction and on-camera tag. As the newscast approaches, it's up to the producer to make sure the director has the script for the live report or at least enough script so he or she can roll a videotape in the report properly. If there is a tape in the live story, make sure it's edited and in place for playback. Don't forget the supers or any graphics.

ENG/SNG receive. In larger stations, engineering will take care of the technical end of working with the microwave or satellite trucks. A technician tells the truck when to transmit and when to power down. That person coordinates between trucks if you are doing more than one live shot. How much time you need between microwave reports can be a production consideration, depending on how your station's microwave is received.

Interviews

Doing any interview live is still one way to get a story. Long ago, however, we learned that many interviews aren't interesting. Interviews must be produced if they are going to be valuable to your viewers. Your talking head needs something important and interesting to say. So, good interviews require planning.

Whom do you interview? The best interviews are with interesting people who have something to say. The only way you can find out is to do a pre-interview. The major morning news shows and the other network interview programs all have people called bookers who arrange interviews. Part of their job is to pre-interview these prospective guests to find out what the interviewee is going to say. In local television, that's your job.

Producing the interview. Don't just allow an interview to happen or allow your anchor do an interview unarmed. Meet with the anchor or reporter and develop a list of questions. Provide background and reference material. Never assume the anchor will read the background. Badger him if you must. You want him to ask good questions, be informed, and to see create a moment in the newscast. If at all possible, find video to include in the lead-in or during the interview. Also consider

TIP
SAFETY

People have been killed operating microwave trucks. Raising and lowering a microwave mast can be dangerous if it gets in power lines. Your responsibility is to make sure that the crew has plenty of time to get to the story and to a safe location. In the event of a breaking story, don't put getting the story on the air ahead of safety. A two-minute jump on the competition isn't worth a human life.

TIP
BE CAREFUL WHEN ORDERING SATELLITE TIME

You're frequently responsible for ordering satellite time. You order this time from your network or from an outside feed service like CNN or CONUS. Because there are several sources of satellite feeds, more than one live shot has been lost because a producer forgot where she ordered the time or didn't get the transponder coordinates right. Take accurate notes and make sure everyone has the correct information well in advance.

graphics, such as a list of key points the interviewee wants to make.

Script the lead-in to the interview carefully. Make sure it tells the viewers why this is an important subject and why they need to watch. In other words, sell the interview. Find the hook that makes this interview important to your viewers. If you can't think of a strong hook, then maybe you should rethink doing this particular interview.

Take care in planning an interview with a hostile subject. Again, arm your anchor or reporter with questions and background material. Make sure she understands this isn't about creating a confrontation. Ask her to start the interview with soft questions before she gets to more confrontational ones. You don't want your anchor to look like she is badgering the poor interviewee even if he's a terrible human being and major league crook. The infamous interview by Dan Rather of then Vice President Bush is an example of how the anchor came out looking mean-spirited even though he asked legitimate questions. Rather's style made Bush look like sympathetic victim.

The ability to report live instantaneously from virtually anywhere in the world and to augment storytelling with computer-created graphics are both reasons today's newscasts are so complex. Graphics and maps are a major part of producing. In other words, if you aren't using graphics properly or aggressively in your newscast, you aren't yet close to being a power producer. The next chapter on graphics gives you a picture of yet one more of your roles as you progress towards becoming a full-fledged power producer.

Chapter 10 — Role Three: Production Expert

Reporting the News with Graphics

In This Chapter:

- Why We Use News Graphics
- Types of Graphics
- Graphics Rules
- Managing News Graphics

Chapter 10: Reporting the News with Graphics

> "Graphics help viewers comprehend a story more quickly and more fully."

If you've been producing or working in a television newsroom for any length of time, you've probably seen your station's still store computer fail. The newscast that night was forced to air with no graphics. It probably looked like half a newscast because graphics are such a part of today's news shows. When a still store fails, it brings home to you just how vital graphics are in creating a television newscast.

This intensive use of graphics makes producing newscasts today dramatically different from even a decade ago. The biggest change came in the early 1980s, when computer-generated graphics, what Quantel called a Paintbox ™, became available.

Combined with the computer still store, computers made graphics easier to create and use. This technology makes the producing job essential because it complicates news production. So, along with the coordination of live reports, stations depend on producers to get a polished broadcast on the air.

Despite this close relationship between producing and graphics, many news producers don't use graphics effectively in their broadcasts. However, power producers understand the purpose of graphics in news. They also know what works and what doesn't, and that making newscasts more visual is an important element of their jobs.

Why We Use News Graphics

There are several good reasons for using graphics in your newscast. First, the style and design of your graphics makes a powerful statement to your viewers about the tone of your news. Second, graphics convey the whole journalistic approach of your news department. For instance, flashy animated graphics like those used in a tabloid-style show say this is an exciting program. More conservative graphics say that this is a straightforward newscast.

No matter what the journalistic approach, stations want to look as though they are contemporary, and management believes graphics help stations make that statement. In fact, some station managers and news directors think a new set and graphics package will somehow improve the ratings. This probably isn't going to happen, but an outdated or inconsistent visual look sends a bad message to viewers. Today's audience has expectations about television production based on what they see on the networks and cable channels. They won't watch channels that don't look current.

Graphics help inform the viewer. Power producers agonize over issues like conversational writing, story structure and story length, all critical to understanding. In creating a newscast you are trying to help your viewers understand the news. Graphics help viewers comprehend a story more quickly and more fully. Power producers understand the value and purpose of graphics.

The most common graphic, besides supers, is the over-the-shoulder (OTS) anchor box. The OTS box gives viewers a quick visual clue about the story. You support the verbal message with a visual punctuation mark. An example would be a picture of a property tax bill with a headline saying, "Property Taxes Increased." Immediately, viewers know this story is about an increase in property taxes. If they own a home, they'll be interested.

Besides the over-the-shoulder boxes, there are other ways to provide visual support for the news, including maps, full-screen lists and animated graphics. The latest generation of computerized graphics can create an almost infinite variety of graphics to illustrate the news. Still, make sure you use graphics as a journalist, to enhance viewer understanding of the news.

Graphics help viewers visualize difficult stories. Stories that were once disregarded or left unreported are now part of a television newscast because graphics can illustrate the key points.

At one time, television news shied away from financial and economic news. Numbers don't make good television, particularly if the only visual support is wallpaper video of the floor of the New York Stock Exchange. Today, you can use computer-generated charts and graphs to illustrate a business story. And those illustrations can be animated to make them even more understandable. The same holds for medical stories and complex investigative reports.

You've probably seen investigative stories where a full-screen graphic helps tell the story. For instance, rather than reading an important document on air, the investigative reporter can use a full-screen graphic with the text.

Graphics help with the pace and flow. Along with saying something about your news vision, visuals help you orchestrate the pace and flow of your newscast. Changing graphics within stories or between stories certainly helps provide a sense of pace. You can develop flow between related stories not only through written transitions but also by maintaining a common graphic. This helps viewers understand that these stories have a common theme. However, remember that a graphic needs to move the story forward; otherwise, don't use it. An inappropriate graphic only confuses the audience.

Types of Graphics

As a producer you have a wide range of graphics to use in your news broadcast. Consider these different forms of visual support, keeping in mind that most of them have a specific job in the newscast.

Logos and bugs. Local stations, cable channels and the networks all have distinctive logos that identify their specific channel easily. These logos are a part of marketing called branding. To stand out in a multi-channel television world, networks and stations must be readily identifiable to the viewer.

WARNING! ACCURACY

You shouldn't have to be reminded that banners need to be reviewed to make certain they are editorially accurate! The story may be great, but if the banner is incorrect or misleading the audience will only remember the mistake.

For example, the CBS eye and the NBC peacock are both powerful brands. Locally, your station uses a logo incorporating the station's channel numbers in a distinctive brand identifier. For a local station this logo can be as powerful as the eye or peacock. During station or channel programming, the logo is converted into a bug and placed on the screen using a keyer device.

While these bugs are often annoying to the viewers, they're

important to your ratings. Given the proliferation of local stations and cable channels, bugs remind viewers which channel they are watching so they can write it down in the all-important Nielsen diary.

Supers. Perhaps the most common graphic you use is a lower third super. Supers superimpose letters over the video picture, thus the name. They're also called CGs, for character generator, the computer used to create them. Supers provide

vital information to the viewers. This could be the name of the person being interviewed a story location or the reporter's name. The second line of a super can be used to further identify an interviewee's job, that person's relationship to the story or a position on an issue.

Labels or banners. Closely related to supers are labels or banners. These provide headlines or other information superimposed over the video picture.

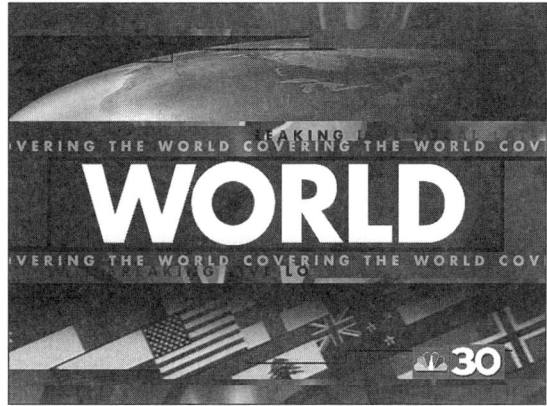

Banners give viewers a visual cue about a story through headlines such as "Mayor Forced to Resign" or "Thousands Flee Hurricane." Banners help your viewers understand the story quickly. Banners also assist newscast pacing, showing the viewer when a story has changed

Labels reinforce a point you want viewers to remember, such as team coverage or continuing coverage of a major story. For instance, a label throughout the medical franchise reminds the viewer that this is "Eye on Health" or "Health Beat." You also use labels to brand major coverage, such as "Team Report" or "Big Story." Labels also go on continuing coverage of a story such as "Flood Crisis 2006" or "Election Y2K."

A banner or label can be a broad super across the lower third of the screen or across an upper corner of the picture. Labels can be done as banners, OTS boxes, or full-screen graphics. The most important role of banners and labels is promotional. No franchise, special report, major coverage or anything else that's important in a newscast should lack a distinctive label. You have to tell the audience what you are doing for them.

Graphic boxes. You're already familiar with the two major types of graphic boxes used in television. The first is the ubiquitous OTS box

behind or beside the anchor or sportscaster. The other is the infamous "dueling boxes," where two separate boxes are created for live reports, interviews or tossing to a reporter on the newsroom flash camera.

In designing graphics for use within OTS boxes, have the artists create a specific graphic with a headline for every story. It isn't acceptable to use a single common graphic for all the stories on the same subject, newscast after newscast. This quickly gets boring.

Using OTS and dueling boxes can cause production problems. Orchestrating camera shots around boxes takes coordination with your director, and depends on how many cameras he has to work with in the studio. Leave enough time in your script for camera movement. In planning your visuals, avoid the possibility of having an anchor read to the wrong camera or some other production error. One of the jobs of a producer is to make your anchors comfortable.

Maps. As you know, television signals cover a large region. Few viewers are familiar with every city, town and village in the DMA. You solve this

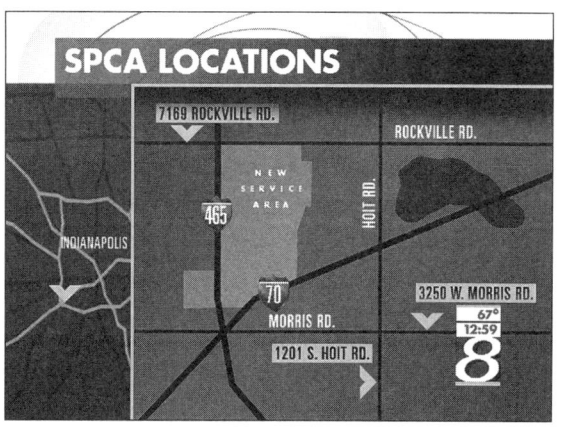

problem by using maps to locate a story for viewers. Viewers relate to news about areas they know, places they've seen, and spots they can locate on a map. Also, maps are invaluable for illustrating stories and helping viewers understand stories better. A good map adds meaning and context to a story.

Designing maps for television news is difficult. You must orient the viewers by showing them something they know, particularly the market's major city. In creating maps, use major cities and interstates and highways before you use county lines to help locate the scene of a story. Avoid political boundaries since most viewers have trouble with boundaries like county lines.

Keep the maps simple and easy to read. Simplify your graphics by limiting the number of items in a map, particularly if it's an OTS box. Full-screen maps are the easiest to read.

Informational graphics. Like maps, most graphics in a newscast provide information. While graphics enhance virtually any story, complex stories demand more graphic support. For instance

graphs, charts, telephone numbers and full-screen lists are just some of the ways to make a complicated story understandable.

Try to use a graphic any time you present information that directly involves the viewer. For instance, in a product recall story, use a picture of the product, or even better, hold up a sample,

>
> **WARNING! BE SPECIFIC**
>
> In designing graphics for video boxes, make sure you are quite specific with the artist about what you need in the design. Remember, most graphic artists aren't journalists and probably don't pay close attention to the news. Faulty instructions on your part can lead to on-air embarrassment. For instance, a graphic of a Boeing 747 crashing with the headline "Airplane Crash Kills One" is pretty silly if the story is about the crash of a single-engine Cessna.

along with a super of the product number and any telephone numbers for the manufacturer or consumer agency. Another example would be any time police are looking for someone in a crime. Get a police sketch along with all the pertinent information on the person they're looking for.

Graphics Rules

Based on their experience, power producers and television graphic artists have developed a set of rules for using graphics within a newscast. Use these rules as you create your rundown and as you work with reporters and the production team before the newscast.

Keep it simple. News viewers can only absorb so much information from the television screen. This means graphics have to be relatively simple in both design and content. If a graphic is too complicated, the viewer will be confused and the graphic won't get the job done. A complicated graphic may look great on a big expensive control room monitor but terrible on home screens. How good is your television at home? Is it properly tuned? The control room picture is crisp and clear, the color properly adjusted, unlike most TV sets in homes. Design graphics for that poorly adjusted home screen.

Keep in mind a rule advertisers use for billboards. No highway billboard is supposed to make more than five main points. The copy must be simple and clear so a driver can understand the message in a few seconds. The same rule applies to television news graphics. The television news audience only has a few seconds to absorb the information.

Beware abbreviations. In creating graphics and supers, be careful to use only easily understood standard abbreviations. Never make up an abbreviation. At one time character generators were limited in the number of letters they could get on a line, so producers and production assistants were guilty of creating unfortunate abbreviations to make the lines fit. Some of those abbreviations did make their way to the air. For instance, in a lower third super for an assemblyman, "Ass." There are countless examples of such sloppy work.

Be consistent. Today stations and networks all make a major investment in the way their newscasts look on the air. A consistent graphics look is an important factor in branding, creating an easily identifiable style to suit your target audience. When viewers tune in to a channel or station they can immediately identify the newscast by its graphic look. Stations now go to outside designers, like Egad! and Television by Design, two companies that create a complete visual look. Egad! even targets specific demographics with its designs. No design detail is overlooked, from the font used to the font size. The designer specifies the exact colors for the station's graphics, the news graphics and the news set.

To ensure that every producer in the news department uses the package properly, the designers give the station a graphics manual. It includes rules with examples on how every on-air graphic should look. You have no, zero, nada, creative room when it comes to working with a design package. Learn and follow the book exactly or you might get yelled at by a manager who paid a lot of money for that graphics package. You've been warned!

Use animation wisely. Animated graphics add to the pacing, create a sense of energy and draw viewer's attention to important newscast elements. A good design package includes animated treatments for key elements of the newscast, like major franchises, the openings for news, weather and sports, and the video bumps before commercial breaks. Another way to get action and energy into your news graphics is to make sure lists are presented as a reveal. In other words, if there are five key points in a report, reveal them line by line, point by point. This is easier to understand and visually interesting.

Watch the screen time. The need for audience understanding governs how long a graphic or super should be on screen. There isn't any specific rule on screen time but visual information must be on the screen long enough for the viewer to fully read the information. Too often supers aren't held on air long enough.

Producers either have short attention spans or are so busy they don't pay attention to this problem. The same can be said for directors and technical directors. This causes what might be called the subliminal super, a super that's on the screen for a fraction of a second. Viewers are confused and cheated of important information. At one station, trying to solve the subliminal super problem, the producer read the super aloud, slowly, in the control room, before the director could take the super off the air. It worked.

Managing News Graphics

You are responsible for getting graphics, and lots of them, in your newscast. For you, the creative part is not in making the graphics—you're not an artist—but managing the process of creating the newscast graphics.

Here are some ideas on how you can better supervise this part of the producing process.

Use a team approach. Make graphic artists full members of your team. Artists need to understand what you are trying to accomplish in that day's newscast. Include them in the morning and afternoon news meetings. Also, set up a separate meeting to deal with graphics. It should include the art director or artist and the newscast director.

When assigning stories to news writers, talk over the graphic potential of that story with them. Make sure they include any graphics already ordered. Of course, the rundown should clearly indicate any visuals planned for that story, such as an over-the-shoulder still store.

Always talk to reporters when they call in after covering a story. One of your major concerns in that conversation has to be graphics. Find out what they think they need in the way of visual support and suggest additional ideas they may have overlooked.

Check and double check. Before completing and publishing your rundown, go over the

---

TIP: KNOW THE EQUIPMENT

When it comes to trying new graphics or innovative and complex production ideas, too often technicians say you can't do something and blame it on the production equipment. Learn the capabilities of your switcher, still store, Paintbox and character generator. Know what you can expect from these tools to use them to their full capacity. Don't allow yourself to be talked out of a good idea because you don't know the equipment.

graphic opportunities in every story. Ask questions. Does this story need a map? How about a full-screen reveal on the key points of a proposed bill? Do the artists need to create an animated label for a special story? Look at that day's coverage for unique stories requiring labels and banners such as "Team Coverage" or "Big Story."

Keep the station's brand in mind. In managing this process, power producers know and understand the overall graphics design for the station. They keep consistency in mind and make sure their graphics keep with station graphics guidelines. Along with the art director, producers perform the function of an enforcer for graphics consistency.

By now, you should have a good idea of what is expected of you on the production end. But don't let your learning end there. Newscast production is constantly evolving. New technology, such as digital television, presents new opportunities to do an even better newscast. For instance, using digital technology, you may be able to segment a newscast to serve different regions within a DMA. Or consider what computers have contributed to movie special effects. That technology can be used to create more informative and understandable television news. No matter what the technology, certain basics will always be part of newscasts, particularly effective news graphics combined with powerful storytelling.

Now you move on to one of your most difficult roles, writing teases that grab and hold the viewers. Virtually every producer struggles with writing good teases every newscast. However, a producer who writes consistently strong teases is invaluable. And a producer who writes these teases and knows where they belong in the newscast is a power producer.

Chapter 11

Role Four: Promotion Writer

Teases that Sell

In This Chapter:

- Positioning Your Newscast
- Enticing Viewers
- Writing Teases that Sell
- Different Teases Do Different Jobs
- Types of Teases
- The Honest Sell

Chapter 11: Teases that Sell

"Tease stories that directly touch the lives of as many viewers as possible."

You're watching the local news when, just before a commercial, the anchor says something inept like, "Stay tuned" or "We'll be right back." What's your reaction? You may work in television but you're no different than most viewers. You grab the remote control and start clicking around to see what else is on. You may have every intention of tuning back to the local news, but a story on CNN, a game on ESPN, or even an old movie on AMC gets your attention. You get hooked and never tune back to the newscast.

A bad tease cost that newscast a viewer. More important, a bad tease may have cost that newscast a ratings point, and that lost ratings point can cost a station hundreds of thousands of dollars.

Weak, ineffective teases plague television news because producers lack the ability to write and produce effective teases. They don't really fully understand that teases are a critical part of their responsibilities. Instead, they write a tease without knowing why viewers should be interested in a story. Or they put off tease writing until the last minute and then write a boring headline.

Power producers don't treat teases as an afterthought or write bad teases. In this chapter you'll learn everything a power producer knows about tease writing: how teases and station promotion are linked and how both contribute to a station's success; how to write teases that entice your viewers to keep watching; and how to keep your teases honest.

Positioning Your Newscast

Teases are actually promotional or marketing copy. In a sense, you're doing the same job as a producer in the promotion department. You're trying to keep viewers watching but at the same time you're building a long-term relationship with the audience. In writing teases it's vital that you understand what your station is trying to accomplish in its news marketing campaign. Your teases need to be consistent with that campaign. If you are "Live, Local, and Late-Breaking" then you tease stories that match this promotional theme.

Promotion and the news. Most successful stations live and breathe their news image. You've seen stations that tie themselves completely to their local news programs. Some stations have even changed their call letters to bring home their commitment, such as Charlotte's WCNC-TV, for Carolina's News Channel and Denver's KCNC-TV, for Colorado News Channel.

These stations are making a position statement about their news. A position statement means defining for the customers, in your case local viewers, the benefits of your news compared to other channels. There are several different positions stations can take in marketing their news. A station can provide the best coverage, or have the most trusted or liked anchor team, or the most contemporary style. Promotion lines like "Live, Local, and Late-Breaking" refer to coverage while "The Team to Turn To" points to news personalities.

As a producer you need to understand this idea of market position. Your job is to create newscasts consistent with your station's position. The news content, the pace and flow, the writing, the anchors' styles, and the style and tone of your teases are all part of delivering a station marketing position.

Enticing Viewers

Teases perform several functions. First, teases get viewers to tune in to the newscast. Second, teases keep those viewers already watching your news from changing channels. The third job for teases is to provide a road map, so viewers know what to expect during the newscast.

Teases get viewers to tune in. The first role of teases is an important one. Your station invests a significant amount of commercial time in promoting your news. Can you imagine the value of a 30-second local news spot during Oprah or another popular show? This is just one reason you must take writing teases as an important daily task.

Teases get viewers to stay tuned. Holding viewers is another critical role for teases. By now you know ratings are extremely important and that the financial well-being of your station is directly tied to ratings. Effective teases are critical to improving the ratings of your newscast. As you know from your own viewing habits, keeping viewers is difficult in this age of the remote control. The best way to keep viewers tuned in is through teases that give them solid reasons for staying with your newscast.

Teases tell viewers what to expect when. Teases provide a road map of what your viewers can expect next in the newscast. However, it's not as simple as just teasing the next story. There is an art to which story to tease and where to tease it in your newscast. For instance, one of the reasons your kicker story is important is its value in trying to keep viewers through the sports block. In fact, you may tease the kicker three or four times in an hour newscast: in the pre-show teases, at the end of the A block, before sports, and again at the end of sports.

Writing Teases that Sell

The first thing you have to do in writing a tease is identify a story with a benefit for the viewers. This means you need to understand your market and the specific audience your newscast serves. What's important to your viewers? What are the gut issues they want to know about? Which stories will they be talking about at the breakfast table or in the office?

Viewer benefit. To keep viewers tuned in, a tease has to provide a reason to stay tuned. The best reasons include a specific, actionable benefit for the viewer.

BAD: "The City council voted last night to increase the property tax. More on that story next"

BETTER: "Your property taxes are going up. We'll tell you by how much and what you can do to fight back...next".

Wide impact. Tease stories that directly touch the lives of as many viewers as possible. This is one reason a specific weather tease works so well. Weather touches everyone and it's something viewers need to know.

Different Teases Do Different Jobs

Once you've decided which stories to tease, you have to decide which type of tease you want to use and why, because different types of teases accomplish different purposes.

Pre-show tease. This type of tease was once a headline, like a newspaper headline. This is your first opportunity to convince the viewers that there are dozens of good reasons for staying tuned. The pre-show tease should tease the big story of the newscast, as well as other important news. Also include an important franchise, the top story in weather or sports, and end with a tease for the show closer.

BAD: *"Next on First at Five:*
- "The abandoned Macy's department store building is on fire. We'll have a live report.
- "Price Cutter opens a new supermarket.
- "Snow in the weather forecast.

TIP
ANALYZE YOUR OWN NEWSCAST

Where you need to tease certain newscast segments dictates where you place stories in your newscast. Take a typical newscast and look at each tease and where the story itself ran. One way to visualize the relationship between teases and the story they promote is this wheel created by Nancy Valenta, executive producer of Fox-owned KTTV in Los Angeles. KTTV places its teases carefully to hold the audience across each break and to the end of the newscast.

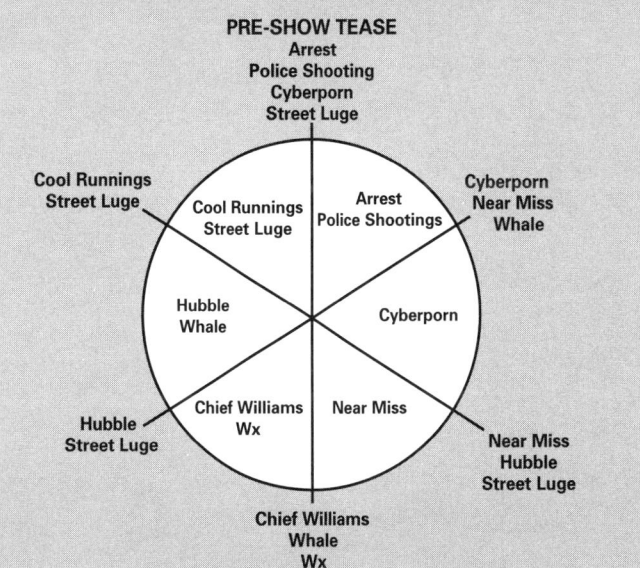

■ "Street luge on ice. That story and more on First at Five."

These are newspaper-style headlines. The basic stories sound interesting but the writing is lackluster and there's no viewer benefit.

BETTER: *"Next on First at Five:*
■ "A downtown landmark you know well...is on fire at this hour. We'll have live reports and we'll tell you how to avoid the traffic mess.
■ "The latest on the local supermarket wars and how you can save money.
■ "Get out that snow shovel...Sally will tell you about a big storm headed our way.
■ "Plus...you won't believe this one even when you see it. Next...on First at Five on Nine."

Next story tease. You start the newscast with a tease and end each newscast block with a tease for the next story after the break. This is a basic rule. Give the audience a reason to stay tuned through the commercials. When teasing several stories, make the last story teased the next story after the commercials. Always run the story you teased as the first story of the next block. Viewers get upset if they have to wait through several stories before they see the story you teased.

Deep teases or superteases. Along with teasing across a commercial break, give viewers reasons to stay tuned for stories later in the newscast. These are called deep teases. These teases hold viewers through segments they may not find as interesting. Deep teases or superteases are important in any newscast but particularly valuable in a longer, one-hour newscast. This is a highly produced tease, with video, live reporters and devices for getting the audiences' attention, like music and animated video.

The kicker tease. Of course the most important tease in your newscast is the tease for the kicker or closer story. This story should always be part of a "deep tease." This tease gets your viewers to stay tuned all the way to the end of the

> **TIP**
> **UNDERSTANDING BEFORE YOU WRITE**
>
>
> Sit down and go over a story you intend to tease to make sure you understand it clearly. Talk to the reporter. You need to know the key points of the story and specific reasons viewers will be interested. Also, remember that stories change. The story you discussed in the morning news meeting may change dramatically by the time it reaches your newscast. Make sure the tease is accurate.

newscast, including viewers who don't like sports.

Next show tease. Another type of tease is the tease delivered at the end of the newscast. Always tease the next broadcast. In fact, no newscast should end without giving viewers a reason to watch your station's next news program. The idea is that if your viewers liked your early newscast, then they'll probably come back to watch the late news. But you need to promise and deliver a story with a viewer benefit.

Topical promos. There is yet another type of tease that you may be responsible for writing. These are the topical promotional teases that run in other programs or in the 3-second station identification spots between programs. These "IDs" are hard to write because you have only a few seconds to deliver the message. They take time and attention. You are trying to attract viewers who watch your station but don't watch your news.

Types of Teases

Writing teases that entice viewers to stay tuned isn't easy. The number of bad teases you hear every day on your own station certainly attests to just how difficult it is to write good teases.

Like reporters, most news producers are trained as journalists. You're taught to report the news, to give the viewers the facts, all the facts. Writing headlines comes naturally to producers and reporters, and is more comfortable than writing promotional copy. You feel uneasy when you deliberately don't include all the information in a sentence.

A headline is actually a short news story. In a single sentence, a headline provides the audience with most of the key details of a story. After hearing a headline the viewer should fully understand the basics of a story. A tease is different. You provide only a part of the story, just enough to create viewer interest. A headline is about providing news; a tease is about promotion.

Headline: "The city council voted last night

to increase property taxes next year by 3 percent. More on that story in a moment." That's a headline. You've given the audience most of what they want and need to know. There is now no compelling reason to stay tuned to hear a story about yet another tax increase.

Tease: "A tax increase ahead...what will it cost you? We'll tell you...next on First News at Five."

There are a variety of ways to approach writing effective teases. Creative tease-writing ranges from making a promise to dramatic video with natural sound. What follows are some ways you can approach writing teases. Try them all. A single tease style bores the audience.

Mystery teases. You create a sense of mystery when you write a tease that leaves out part of the story. These teases leave the audience interested but wondering what the story is all about. You do need to give enough important information to let the audience know the story is important. Resist the temptation to mislead your viewers. A misleading tease might say something like "Sexual predator loose," with no hint the story is thousands of miles away! Example: "Your city council has some bad news for taxpayers...next."

Question teases. Perhaps the most common tease style is the question. The question can be aimed at a viewer benefit or at a powerful emotion. Used too often, questions sound manipulative and contrived. Example: "What kind of man could set fire to a home with a mother and child inside?"

Promise teases. Creating teases that promise a viewer work well. In this type you create anticipation of a benefit such as special, relevant information on a story with direct viewer impact. Example: "A major recall of minivans. We'll tell you which minivans are involved and what you'll need to do if you own one...next."

Video teases. Television is about dramatic, exciting or funny video. People tune in to television news to see the news so memorable video makes a great tease. Tell your viewers what they are going to see, show them a hint of the video, but don't give it away. Example: (snow storm video of a car sliding into and knocking down a police officer helping another motorist) "...a close call for a local police officer...next."

Natural sound or sound bite teases. Along with great pictures, great sound really captures the audiences' attention. A sound bite of dramatic emotion or a strong statement can make the viewers take notice. Sound used properly encourages the audience to stay tuned.
Example: "A big Fourth of July spectacular..." (sounds of fireworks...boom, boom, boom).

Exclusives. News viewers watch the news because they want to be informed and they like being the first to know something. A highly effective tease promises the audience they'll see something in your newscast they won't see elsewhere. The best teases of this type include great video. Example: Only on Two...exclusive pictures (not film, tape or video) of chaos at the county fair...next on First at Five. Another way of saying "exclusive" is to use a line such as "Only on Two" or "seen here first." Don't imply that a story is exclusive if it isn't. To do so only gets the audience mad.

Timely teases. News by definition is timely. Viewers want to see the news just as soon as possible. Referring to the time element is a good technique to use in writing teases. Example: "Just moments ago, a new disclosure in the case of a taxpayer fighting city hall for you...next on Five."

Personalized teases.

TIP
LIVE TEASES

Live teases from the scene of the big story or a taped reporter tease are extremely effective and remind the viewers that your newsroom is working hard to get them the latest news. However, there is a problem when reporters write their own teases. Too often reporters deliver headlines that give most of the story. Review the reporters' tease copy just as carefully as you review their actual news reports.

TIP
TARGET YOUR TOPICAL PROMOS

When writing teases and promotional copy that run in entertainment programs outside the newscast, keep the audience for that specific program in mind. Find stories to tease that are interesting to that show's demographic. If it is a women-oriented talk show, you don't want to tease a big sports story but instead a story on women's health or a consumer investigation.

WARNING!
DON'T CHEAT THE VIEWERS

Compelling video is a surefire audience draw. Just remember you then have to deliver a complete story, not just a few seconds of exciting video. Never cheat the viewers by just repeating the same video used in your tease. The audience deserves the full story.

Aim your tease language directly at the viewer benefit. Write your teases so the audience understands you are bringing them valuable information, information they want and need, news that touches their lives. Use language that refers directly to the viewer. The word "you" makes a direct statement that this story involves the viewer. Example: "You'll pay more to city hall...and we'll tell you how your neighbors are fighting back... next on Action News.

Tease clichés. Much tease writing is done by rote. It's almost as though producers have a template in their brain and can't deviate. It's a process of "plug in teases." Plug-in teases don't work because viewers don't listen to teases they've heard a thousands times. Example: "The city council raises property taxes...details when we come back."

Tease language. In writing teases, the power producer strives for action verbs and present tense. With only a few seconds to convey the message, effective tease need powerful words. Every tease should contain a verb, and that verb should be memorable. Example: The city council hits homeowners in the pocketbook...what you can do to battle back...next.

Remember your anchor. Some anchors are superb tease writers, but many are not. Most anchors start as reporters and are trained as journalists. They have a tough time not writing a news headline. Therefore, the job falls to you as the producer. But in writing teases for your anchor, remember to write in his or her style. By matching the anchor's style you'll write more effective teases because they can sell the tease with their delivery.

The Honest Sell
Some broadcast journalists look down at writing

WARNING! DEADLY DETAILS

There are certain mistakes done every day in television news that should never happen. The biggest mistake tease writers make is the use of the odious word "details." The word is boring and obvious. If you're reporting the news then you are supplying the details of a story.

teases. They feel that writing promotion copy is beneath them. Actually, writing teases is as important as anything else in the newscast. Teases need to be journalistically sound. A tease may be promotional material but every tease must be accurate and fair.

Don't use tabloid language. Tabloid shows try to draw viewers with drama and emotion. This is fine as long as the information is accurate, but too often these teases step over the line. "City in mourning for a fallen star" goes for the emotional hook. It's a broad statement and the writers don't have any idea if the entire city is in mourning! Power producers don't write dishonest teases or those that exploit people.

Never mislead your viewers. Don't write a tease that can mislead viewers. People don't like to be fooled. In fact, misleading teases are a major complaint about local television news. Example: "Deadly plane crash...tape at eleven." It sounds like a major crash but the story is about a single-engine private plane and the pilot is dead. This story is no more important than a fatal traffic accident. Your viewers probably don't care.

Take the time to write good teases. Never leave tease-writing until the last minute. Writing against your newscast deadline means you are going to create forgettable and ineffective teases. Writing teases is difficult. It takes your time and attention. This task is not an afterthought for a power producer.

Writing a good tease is a challenge, but there's another producer role that's even more demanding and time-consuming. That role is leading a team. Creating a newscast takes a team, and you're a leader of this team. In the next two chapters you'll learn about the people and leadership skills that power producers master to become team leaders.

Chapter 12

Role Five: Team Leader

Coaching Your Team

In This Chapter:

- What Is a Team?
- Team Leadership
- Team Goals
- Personal Style
- Work Types
- The Anchor as Team Member

Chapter 12: Coaching Your Team

"You may feel better after venting your frustration but you won't solve problems playing the blame game."

For the third time this week, your newscast suffered a major meltdown, an on-air disaster. A story wasn't edited in time to make its proper slot in your show. The news director is upset, the anchor is upset and you're upset. How can this keep happening? Whose fault is it?

You can play the blame game or you can solve the problem. Most producers prefer the blame game; it's easy. You may feel better after venting your frustration but you won't solve problems playing the blame game. And the blame game doesn't build teamwork.

Creating television news is a team sport. Power producers understand that getting a television newscast on the air smoothly, without mistakes, takes teamwork. To create a consistently excellent newscast requires producers with exceptional leadership skills.

In this chapter you'll learn what it takes to be a team leader. You'll learn about teams and teamwork. You'll discover why team goals are so important. You'll learn how you and the other members of the team approach your jobs. And you'll learn how to handle a sometimes difficult relationship, the one between the anchors and the rest of the news team. You'll be pleased to know that you can build a productive working relationship with a news anchor!

What Is a Team?

As a news producer, you are a member of several teams, but the most important team is the one that creates your newscast. Each member of the team needs to do his or her job well for that newscast to be successful.

TEAM. The idea behind a team is best summed up in an acronym used by Roger Penske, known both for his winning auto racing team and his success as a businessman. Penske's acronym is:
- **T**ogether
- **E**veryone
- **A**chieves
- **M**ore

In other words, a team, working together, can accomplish far more than an individual working alone.

When is a team a team? Just calling a work unit a team doesn't make it one. Creating a real team is a major part of your job. You need to create a team with individuals from different departments with varied skills and work styles. You also have to do this in a business that doesn't traditionally recognize that newscast production takes a team.

Your team members don't all come from the same department. They come from production, engineering, graphics and news. This is called a cross-functional team and represents a difficult situation. Typically, they don't see themselves as part of a team but rather as just doing a job. In fact, many of those on your team aren't fully aware of all the steps in the news process. They only see their part in getting the newscast on the air. An example is reporters who have no idea what they've done to the newscast when their story runs too long or is not edited on time.

The team attitude. Teams start with attitude. You're a team member if you think of yourself as part of a team and work together with others to achieve common goals. Given good leadership, team members who understand the newscast process and the role they play in that process develop a team attitude.

Another way to develop team attitude is thinking in terms of a process and group responsibility. It helps to end the blame game and build a sense of mutual understanding. Because they see the process, team members support each other, regardless of department, to fashion the best possible newscast.

POWER PRODUCER: A PRACTICAL GUIDE TO TV NEWS PRODUCING

Team Leadership

The toughest part of leading a team for a news producer is that you aren't the boss. You may be responsible for news content and planning the newscast but you have little formal power. For a task-driven newscast producer this is a major test of leadership skills.

Without formal power over some team members, improving the newscast process takes careful and smart leadership. Since you aren't the boss but still have goals to achieve, this means you've got to find another way for your team to reach these goals. You do this by becoming a coach. This doesn't mean behaving like a football coach who stands on the sidelines and swears. You coach through using assertive management skills like clear and open communication, listening, questioning and offering specific feedback. What do you do to become a coach and team leader?

Understand. The coaching leader works to understand each individual on the team. He develops personal relationships. The coach understands team members' work styles, their emotional level, their professional skills and their personal needs. Each team member is a real person to this coach.

Communicate. A coach develops a bond with team members by communicating clearly and candidly. There can be no secrets or hidden agendas between team and coach. If the news is bad, the team needs to know. If there is an honest reason the team can't be given information, such as audience research on the anchors, then they need to know that.

Be candid. A candid relationship means being honest and open with your team members. If you're open and honest, there will be fewer misunderstandings or misinterpretation. What is amazing is how few newsroom managers have the confidence or skill to be candid.

Be clear. Producers don't always communicate clearly. It's not that they can't communicate, the problem is failing to think through the message and form it properly. Power producers take a few seconds to stop, look directly at someone and communicate a complete thought. Then they make sure the message has been received and understood.

Question carefully. Intelligent and careful questioning is vital to the coaching process. Rather than jumping to a quick conclusion, use questions to get at the heart of the issues. How can you lead if you can't accurately define the problem or situation? As a producer/reporter, you should already have some sense of how to ask good questions. Like a reporter, start with open-ended questions aimed at a broad understanding. Ask who, why, what, when, where and how questions. Then zero in on the specific issues. Avoid unproductive closed-end and judgmental questions. A judgmental question can quickly destroy a productive discussion.

Listen. To be understood, you first need to listen. Unfortunately, few producers take time to listen properly. Given the hectic pace of the news production process this isn't surprising. Listening is hard work, but it is something you can learn and practice. Here are some ways you can make sure you understand the other person's message:

- Meet away from the distractions of a busy newsroom. Use a private office, conference room or edit booth if necessary.
- Even if this is a hurried conversation in the

TIP
ASK WHY

One way to get to the heart of a problem is to keep asking **why** until you've peeled the problem back to its core. Often the surface issue is a symptom and not the core issue the team actually needs to solve.

For example:

"Why was the tape late for its slot in the show?"
"The script didn't get to the edit booth until the show was already on the air."
"Why was the script late?"
"The reporter couldn't get started on it until a half hour before air."
"Why was the reporter so late in getting back to the station?"
"We got lost trying to get to the story and someone took our map book from the news car."

This drill is a start at finding the real problem that helped cause the late tape. Of course there are other **why** questions you could ask in this scenario and probably more than one issue involved! Keep asking **why** and you stand a better chance of getting to the real problems.

newsroom, set aside what you are working on and concentrate on the person talking. This isn't just a matter of being polite; it's part of understanding.

■ Focus your attention on the listening process. Don't allow your mind to wander or spend your time trying to think of a response. If necessary, take notes but look at the other person.

■ Don't prejudge either the message or the person delivering the message even if you haven't always had the best relationship. Keep an open mind.

■ Deal first with the ideas and facts. Are there sufficient facts to back up what is being said? Ask questions to get specific information.

■ Take your time in responding. Don't try to answer a point or form a response while listening. Make sure you've heard the other person through. Don't interrupt just because you've had a great idea. Keep quiet.

■ Watch carefully for nonverbal cues. Probably 80 percent of communication is nonverbal. Reading body language, gestures and other visual clues is critical to understanding the message.

■ Avoid the blame game. Remember that you're interested in solving problems, not affixing blame. If the other team member starts to slip into this popular but toxic newsroom routine, use questions to get him or her back on track.

■ Avoid the accusatory "you should" favored by aggressive managers. To launch a discussion of a problem this way makes people defensive and just starts the blame game. You don't solve problems by personal attacks.

Give constructive feedback. To have clear communication, strong teamwork and a successful newscast, you must give feedback. A major part of leadership is providing constructive feedback. Too often, well-intentioned feedback becomes criticism and blame. Instead of communicating, the team member becomes defensive and hostile. As with listening, constructive feedback deals with specific issues. It involves open-ended questions and getting at facts. Use questions to get team members to look at the reasons they may be letting the rest of the team down.

Praise and recognition of someone's accomplishments, given honestly and quickly, goes a long way toward reinforcing a job well done. All of us want to keep doing something that is viewed by managers and our peers as a good thing.

Team Goals

In order to have constructive communication and teamwork, your news team needs specific goals. They need to know what they are trying to accomplish. Without a goal, a team is just a collection of people who show up every day in the newsroom to put a newscast on the air. How can you judge someone's performance, or your own, if your team isn't working toward a meaningful and valuable goal?

Create goals for the team. Your primary task as a team leader is to help develop goals for your team. A team goal, sometimes called a vision, is a future objective everyone on the team can work toward. Every process must have short-term, tactical goals, but a team also requires long-term, strategic goals. The best goals urge the team to do something that they can see has real value for the team, its members, the station and the audience. Valid goals stretch the skills and resources of your team but acknowledge limitations like budgets and equipment.

Setting goals is a team process, so setting a goal doesn't mean announcing to everyone that they have a goal. The team has to help create the goal and understand why the goal is important. This means honestly communicating the facts.

Make sure the goals are specific and measurable. For a goal to be vital, it must be specific, measurable, important and doable within a given time frame. For example, if you are still in school, getting an A this semester in a class important to your future is a specific, short-term goal. As a producer your goal might be having one promotable enterprise story in your newscast every day within six months. In other words, a goal for your team must be clear, measurable in some way, and something the team believes can be accomplished within a time frame. Your team goal must fit with the overall vision of the news department and the station. If the goal doesn't fit within the vision, it's not valuable.

Example: Your goal might be to attract more viewers in the 18-49 demographic during the November sweeps by creating and starting two promotable franchises in the newscast targeted at that demo before the start of the ratings period. Does this goal meet the criteria? It's specific, important and timely. It can be measured during the November ratings book. After the sweeps you need to share the final ratings so the team knows if its effort paid off. Facilitating the goal-setting process is a major responsibility of leadership.

Set smaller goals along the way. The best way to accomplish a long-range major goal is to set up less difficult, short-range objectives. Too often a team fails to achieve a tough long-range goal because it appears too hard. Your team may give up in frustration. It's far easier to accomplish a tough goal if you cut it up into smaller, easier objectives so it seems less difficult.

Celebrate team accomplishments. Team members work for a sense of accomplishment and recognition. A sense of accomplishment builds a desire to do it again. When your team reaches one of its short-term objectives, observe that success with a team party or individual recognition. There are different things your team can do to celebrate, from ordering special apparel like baseball caps and T-shirts, to a party in the newsroom. Whatever you do, recognize achievement and do it quickly.

Personal Style

To be a team leader you need to understand that everyone manages differently. Your management style is based on a number of factors, including self-image, personal experience and how you see your current work environment.

Unfortunately, few producers actually try to analyze their management style. Most tend to go on instinct and conventional wisdom. This is how bad management habits pass from one generation of producers to the next. Power producers don't rely on instinct and conventional thinking. Instead they work to understand their own strengths and weaknesses in creating a leadership style that works for them.

Manager vs. leader. To learn about your own work approach, you need to know that there's an important distinction between a manager and a leader. Most people in your newsroom, even most news directors, haven't thought about this crucial difference.

Managers accomplish goals and tasks; they get things done. Most producers are managers. They take care of all the details to get a newscast on the air.

Leadership is another skill entirely. Just because you're a good manager doesn't mean you're a leader. Leadership is about setting a goal for an organization and then providing the resources and guidance to reach that goal. Leadership is about having a vision of a better newscast and a better newsroom. Leadership can come from a manager or team member with leadership traits. Those traits include professional skill, trust, personality and the capacity to articulate a sense of direction. The most important leadership trait is the ability to work with other people in a positive working style, a style known as assertive leadership.

Passive	Assertive	Aggressive

Passive producers. A leader's behavior is typically toward one end or another on a scale from passive to aggressive. At one end are passive people who avoid difficult problems and conflict. They try to dodge situations that make them uncomfortable. These producers often appear submissive. This person has a script in his head that says, "I'm not okay, you're okay." This is hardly a good starting point for success as a team leader.

Aggressive producers. At the opposite end of this scale are aggressive producers who take charge of situations and seek control. These producers often don't care what others think or feel just so long as the job gets done. They think the successful completion of a task justifies the means. The aggressive manager has a tape in his head that says, "I'm okay, you aren't okay." This mindset can backfire on the overly domineering manager. People bullied or abused to achieve a short-term result can't be counted on to help in the future. Why kill yourself to edit a tape on deadline for an offensive jerk? An unfortunate tradition in broadcast journalism promotes the idea that you have to be a tough guy, a macho manager, to get the job done. Particularly at the networks, aggressive producers and managers have been encouraged and promoted. Ultimately, many so alienate their colleagues that they fail as leaders.

Assertive producers. Power producers follow a more successful middle way. They manage assertively. This is the best way to achieve your goals in today's newsroom. Assertive producers don't try to overpower others or give up important goals to avoid confrontation. Assertive producers share the following traits:

- They involve the team when facing a problem or making a decision.
- They respect what team members contribute to team success.
- They listen to others instead of talking.
- They question and find facts.
- They don't avoid difficult or unpleasant situations, decisions or people.
- They coach team members to better performance.

The assertive producer has the personal self-confidence and awareness to take advantage of all that members bring to a team. Assertive producers have a positive script, "I'm okay, you're okay." This is the best mind-set to build a team. People want to work for an assertive producer.

Work Types

Along with an assertive approach to working with teammates, you bring your own personal approach to your daily job. This style is the way you work, the way you get your job done. You don't leave your fundamental personality at home when you go to work. Understanding your own approach and that of others on your team makes you a much stronger leader.

Four work types. To predict the way you and each of your team members approach your roles, start with four basic works types loosely based on the personality types identified in the Myers-Briggs Type Indicator test. While this is a simplified way of looking at work patterns, each of us prefers one of these basic approaches and uses it most of the time. You can use this knowledge to gain insight into how each team member will deal with difficult situations.

There are four basic ways people approach their jobs:

- **Taskmaster/Goal-driven:** Wants to get the job done at all cost. Driven to accomplish tasks. Tends to be an aggressive personality.
- **Performer/Ego-driven:** This personality wants to be known. Also more aggressive than passive.
- **People person/Relationship-driven:** Enjoys other people and is an extrovert but can be a passive personality.
- **Never makes a mistake/Perfection-driven:** Wants to get a job completed correctly and is an introvert, often passive.

Know your own work style. Most producers tend to be task-driven; they like to get things done. The negative is that producers are seldom perfectionists. They also like to be in control, and aren't people-oriented. They don't always take the time to recognize people who need or deserve recognition. However, these are generalizations; no one always fits only one approach.

Everyone combines elements of other styles. Power producers realize this and adapt their own approach to getting the job done as the situation and people demand. They understand different work types and modify their behavior to fit the personality of the team member, adapting to suit each individual rather than expecting the team members to adjust to them.

Know what motivates your team. You need to recognize why your team members come to work. It's not about money. Certainly team members work for a paycheck, but every study of why people work puts money down the list. A 1992 survey by Gallup quoted in Robert Half's 1993 book, *Finding, Hiring and Keeping the Best Employees*, lists the most important job characteristics:

- Interesting work
- Job security
- Opportunity to learn new skills
- Vacation of a week or more
- Freedom to work independently
- Recognition from coworkers
- Ability to help others
- Limited job stress
- Regular hours
- High income

Make work challenging and rewarding. This list indicates you'll have more success motivating and leading your team by involving team members in interesting and challenging work. This is why including team members in the goal process is so important.

The Anchor as Team Member

People want the news from people they like, respect and trust. Having news anchors who fulfill those criteria is one of the primary reasons viewers watch a station's news. So it's no surprise that news directors and station management see news anchors as the reason for a station's success or failure.

Because anchors are so important to the newscast, you and your newscast team must make the anchors look good. You have to protect them from the technical and journalistic blunders that can leave them looking bad on the air. For instance, be careful where you place stories with different emotional tones. You create an awkward situation for your anchor if you run a tragic story next to a funny story.

Understand their perspective. There are many complicating factors in the relationship between your anchor and your newscast production team. You need to be aware of these challenges in working with the anchor team. Consider:

- **Age and experience:** The anchors are normally older and more experienced than the producers and most of the rest of the team. Anchors often feel that young producers lack maturity and judgment when it comes to putting together a newscast. This is one of the best reasons for you to remain calm during a crisis. The anchor needs to trust and understand your directions when you tell him what to do next.
- **Work schedule:** Anchors work different hours than the rest of the team so they sometimes have only a limited amount of time to spend on the newscast. For example, station management regularly asks these local personalities to make appearances to promote the news and the station.
- **Location:** While the producers and production team work in the center of the newsroom, the anchors often have offices and are cut off from the news production process.
- **Chain of command:** While the producer is in charge of the newscast, the anchors commonly deal directly with the news director or even with the general manager when they have a complaint or suggestion. This reality can be difficult for producers who don't enjoy the anchor's respect.

Improving the relationship. As team leaders, power producers find ways to involve the anchors in the team and news process.
- Get the anchors to attend meetings.
- Don't let them out of such requirements as having to come up with story ideas every day. Solicit story ideas from your anchors.
- Go over the rundown with the anchors as soon as they arrive for work. Review story placement and why they've been given each particular story to read.
- Have the anchors write their own copy. Knowing the stories and the copy helps them do a better job of delivering that copy.
- Encourage them to work part of the day in the newsroom so they know what is going on.
- Get them a copy of the script for review as early as possible.
- Call the anchors when making a major change or when faced with a potential problem like a late-breaking story.

Encourage anchor involvement. Unfortunately, some producers resent anchors, especially those who jump in with ideas at inopportune times. Rather than fume, get the anchor involved in planning the broadcast. It's tough to second-guess the producer if you've had a hand in the way the show came together. Plus, some anchors actually have excellent ideas that can help the newscast!

The road to becoming a news team both on and off the air is difficult. As a leader you face team conflicts and deal with difficult personalities. Given strong and intense people working against tight deadlines, there are bound to be problems in newsrooms. In the next chapter you'll find out how to cope with conflict and deal with difficult people.

Interview: News Anchor

Demetria Kalodimos
Anchor/Reporter
WSMV-TV
Nashville

Demetria Kalodimos anchors newscasts on WSMV, the NBC affiliate in Nashville. She also does investigative reports, series and documentaries, as well as a regular entertainment feature. She joined WSMV in 1984 as weekend anchor and reporter, and was promoted to primary anchor of the 5 p.m., 6 p.m. and 10 p.m. broadcasts in 1988. She has won numerous AP, IRE and Emmy awards as well as a regional RTNDA Murrow award for a documentary. She began her career at WICD-TV in Champaign-Urbana, IL, after receiving an MS in journalism from the University of Illinois in 1983.

Describe an ideal relationship between a producer and an anchor.

The producer is basically creating the newscast and the anchor is going to deliver that creation to the viewer. If anchors and producers don't work together, something will suffer, either the gathering of the information or the execution of the newscast.

Since you are also a reporter, how do you see the relationship between a producer and a reporter?

Producers have certain expectations coming out of the assignment meeting in terms of where a story is going to play, how it's going to play, and its elements. Frequently a story sounds great that morning but as you pursue it you learn it's not great. Or it might even be better than we knew in the morning meeting.

I hope that most crews communicate with the producer at least once during the day to let him or her know how the story is progressing. The last thing the poor producer needs is a crew walking in and saying they've got nothing a half-hour before deadline.

What do producers do that gets in the way of their relationship with an anchor?

Sometimes producers are so married to the rundown they've created that when a monkey wrench gets thrown, producers can't see past what they've put together.

The only time I clash with a producer is when we have to kill and rearrange stories on the air. Often the producer many not remember there is a transitional sentence in the next story that prevents it from standing alone, or that entire blocks could be moved with better results than just cutting one or two stories in a block.

Often the producer is more sensitive than the anchors to keeping anchor reads even. At the last minute producers say we are going to change the next three stories and who reads them for the sake of keeping things even between anchors. If it's a co-anchored show, I've already reviewed and edited the stories I'm going to read on the air for my own style. If at the last minute you assign me two more stories I haven't read, you end up with a big mess. I would hope when it's hitting the fan and we are rearranging things, producers wouldn't worry about changing the reads and preserving the Ping-Pong match. It would be better to read the stories you're familiar with and wait your turn.

What involvement do you want to have as the show comes together?

No more or less than anyone else around the table. A good example was when we had breaking news about the autopsy results for Tammy Wynette. Everyone was putting in his or her two cents about what should be included. I felt strongly that we needed a thorough package on the sorts of drugs they found in her system. I felt it would be important to have an actual white coat telling what these drugs do and when it's proper to prescribe and administer them. As it turned out, we did do the story I suggested, not for the 6 but the 10. I thought it was the best story of the day in terms of information.

It's not automatic that when an anchor says something it's going to happen and I like that. Our arguments have to be as strong as anyone else's.

What things do producers do that drive you nuts?

Sometimes they give instructions via IFB that are long, wordy and repetitive. I'm trying to break one of our producers of the habit of telling me everything twice: "The next page is dead, repeating, the next page is dead." Often producers don't understand that when they cut in, all other audio cuts out, including that of the reporter in the field who is about to toss to you, the interview subject who is answering the question you just posed, or material in the story you need to hear so you can formulate a coherent question. The longer they talk in your ear, the longer you're tuned out of needed information.

If a producer must talk to the anchor, say something as simple as, "next story" or "no tape" or "take a break." That's all. Most of us who have been doing this for a long time know exactly what to say. You don't have to script it for us. We do better if the producer let's us know what's going on and we can formulate our own words, be it an apology or a quick toss.

What are some of the good things producers do? What sets the best producers apart?

The best producers look at the show as a whole, not just spaces they fill in on a template. They look at the show as a total creation rather than three blocks with two breaks, and weather and sports.

The best producers look for chances to break up long reads with small bits of natural sound. Or they find an unusual structure for a show, such as starting with sound off the top or doing a reopen. They do things that make the show look a little different. They make it visually and aurally more interesting for the audience.

The best producers are the best writers. If they really pay attention to writing good transitions, good clean teases and good headlines, it becomes a pleasure for the anchor to read the show.

What advice would you have for entry-level producers?

Don't buy into the notion that the producer-anchor or producer-reporter relationship is adversarial. In the best shops everyone works as a team. Producers and anchors are good friends even outside the newsroom. The best broadcasts come when people are on the same page and appreciate each other's role on the team but at the same time complement each other.

I had a 10 o'clock producer who is now our news director, and one of the reasons he rose through the ranks so quickly was because of the friendships and good working relationships he forged. For instance, when a story broke he'd call everyone out of their offices and cubicles to the platform where the producers work. We could hear the comments and the spur-of-the-moment ideas about how we should respond. As a result we did great breaking news coverage.

What about the age difference between producers and more experienced anchors?

I don't find that with age comes wisdom and increased skills. I've seen plenty of people who've been in the business a long time who've purposely shut themselves off from new ways to produce stories and the new, cool stuff that's coming along technically. I think it's great when we have fresh new blood who looks at news differently. That's the advantage of having young people straight out of school or in their first or second jobs. At the same time, there's a lot to be learned from the people who know the community, know community standards, how things are done, and what's going to fly and what isn't. I'd say play up the new ideas but at the same time do it in such a way that you are respecting the people who set the standards in your newsroom.

Producers don't get recognized very often. The producer and the director of the newscast are two people you never see, whose names you never hear, and whose names you rarely see at the end of every show.

I don't know how many newsrooms even have credits any more, but it's a nice stroke. It's so exciting to see an assistant producer or someone climbing the ladder and on the first day they get their chance to finish up a show, hopefully on time, and see their name supered at the end. Lots of times everyone in the newsroom applauds if it's that producer's first show. A little thing like credits can mean a whole lot to people who spend their entire day putting sweat and blood into a show but don't really have anything to show for it at the end.

Chapter 13

Role Five: Team Leader

Dealing with Difficult Personalities

In This Chapter:

- The Basics
- Dealing with Your Boss
- Dealing with Office Politics
- Dealing with Difficult People
- Dealing with Team Conflict

Chapter 13:
Dealing with Difficult Personalities

"You can't expect team members to approach the same task with the same mind-set."

Even if you haven't been in television news long, you've probably already been through a difficult situation. An anchor angrily tosses his script at the producer, annoyed because he thinks he didn't have a large enough role in the newscast. A live report doesn't make air because an engineer fails to turn on the microwave receiver on time, getting even with a rude producer. After the microwave failed, a director blows up at a producer.

Conflict in television newsrooms is common, partly because the tension level is so high. Tension is natural with creating a newscast. However, much of your stress also comes from a mix of strong personalities and different work styles. The ability to cope with these and other challenges is an essential skill for all news producers.

In this chapter you'll find basic, proven rules for dealing with difficult people. It offers valuable tips on how to manage your boss and how to succeed at office politics without playing politics. Most importantly, you'll learn specific strategies to work with troublesome personalities and how to resolve team conflicts so you can create a winning newscast.

The Basics
As a producer and team leader you try to create a productive working relationship, one that contributes to getting your newscast on the air. Your goal is to get every team member to contribute fully to the newscast process. That's the most important thing. People are only difficult if their actions get in the way of the news process.

Remember the different work types. First, you know that each of us favors one of four basic work types. You can't expect team members to approach the same task with the same mind-set. As you learned in the last chapter, no work style is better than another. Work style means you and your team members bring different values, energy and perceptions to the news process. This isn't good and it isn't bad; it's workplace reality.

Keep your newsroom goals first. The healthiest way to deal with problem people and conflict is to keep your long-term goals firmly in mind. It's easy to get off your priorities when someone is behaving like a jerk. However, if it has nothing to do with what you are trying to accomplish, then don't get involved. Getting sidetracked in a pointless debate or a temper tantrum is a waste of your time. Teams work best and are the most valuable when they are working toward specific goals. A team leader keeps the team focused on those goals despite obstacles. Some of the most difficult obstacles for a team are people problems. Don't let significant goals slip away as your team copes with people issues.

You can be difficult, too. Also understand that at different times and in different ways everyone can be difficult. You don't like to think about it but you have your own work type. Your experience, personality and limitations can make you difficult at times. With this knowledge, you can compensate for your shortcomings.

Dealing with Your Boss
Perhaps there is not a more difficult newsroom relationship than the way you work with your boss. A successful producer manages this crucial relationship. What does managing your boss mean? It sounds manipulative but means understanding how to meet her needs, and to do so in a way that's compatible with her work style.

Understand your boss' goals. Try to understand what your boss actually wants to accomplish. Often, it's up to you to figure out her goals. Some news directors and executive producers aren't clear or can't articulate how they want things done. If you can't figure out what they are trying to do then you are going to have to ask them. Never rely on newsroom gossip.

Understand your boss' work style. As you know, you have your own work style and so does your boss. Unfortunately, she seldom tells you how she likes things done so you'll have to figure out her work type. Some bosses like memos with lots of facts and some want to see you in person and talk things over. In any event, you have to understand her approach to work and successfully adapt to it.

Trust is essential. There's a special relationship between you and your boss. Her success depends in some measure on your success. Just as you depend on her for direction and resources, she needs you to execute your job properly. You need to accomplish your part of the overall goal. Mutual trust with your boss is critical to this relationship. If you don't trust your boss or your boss doesn't trust you, then bad things happen. A boss who doesn't trust an employee may not communicate well with that employee or give her enough room to make important decisions.

Keep your boss informed. Let your boss know what's going on and how your team is doing. She may not be aware of how much progress you've made on your team goals. It's up to you to keep her informed, and in a way she'll find comfortable.

Dealing with Office Politics

Managing your relationship with your boss is one part of office politics. It's smart to manage not only your relationship with your boss but all your relationships in the station and newsroom. While office politics is often seen as a negative, if you manage the relationships it doesn't have to be.

Listen to the grapevine. Most managers view office politics as spending too much time passing along information on that informal communication channel known as the grapevine. Unfortunately for managers, the grapevine is not about to go away. In fact, smart managers and power producers tap into as many different sources of information as possible. It's important for you to regularly take the newsroom temperature, to find out what is going on and how situations are perceived. Don't take every comment or judgment as true, but listen to do a better job as a team leader.

Avoid being a gossip. While keeping in touch with the grapevine, avoid being a gossip. Spreading gossip is unproductive. News managers tend to see gossips as people who spot problems but don't have answers, whiners. They'll never be power producers because they don't solve problems.

Avoid cliques. On your first or second day in a new station you'll probably be asked to go to lunch or to get a cup of coffee. This is your introduction to the grapevine and often it's the first step to joining a clique. Get that coffee but be careful. The first people to approach you in your new job will probably be the malcontents and whiners. Don't get sucked in and never limit yourself to one group of associates in the newsroom.

Develop trust. Rather than joining a clique, develop relationships with colleagues in the newsroom in terms of trust. The teamwork needed to get a newscast on the air is built on respect and trust. If it's not there, the tension level in your newsroom will escalate into conflict and personality clashes. A lack of trust leads to unproductive political games in your newsroom.

Don't play political games. The most significant and disruptive part of office politics is political games. Typically these games develop when someone sets out to achieve a personal goal at the expense of others. For example, it's a political game when a producer decides to sabotage an anchor she doesn't like by trying to make that anchor look bad, or when an anchor takes her complaints about a producer directly to the general manager. Any conduct in the workplace that isn't honest, open or in the best interest of the entire newsroom is unproductive. Ultimately, political games don't work.

Dealing with Difficult People

People who play newsroom politics are just one of the many types of difficult people who make up a news staff. Sometimes you will have to deal with people who put their own interests and needs ahead of all else. At other times you will be confronted with people who are insecure or fearful about their ability to do the job. There are all kinds of reasons for difficult behavior and the cause isn't always apparent.

Over the years the people involved in getting your newscast on the air have found methods for dealing with problems and situations. They've learned that bullying intimidates or that saying as little as possible helps them get their own way. For instance, the anchor who feels threatened by changes in the show will lash out at the producer to gain control of the situation. People use difficult behavior because they've learned it gets results.

The way people behave when being difficult depends on work type, whether they are taskmasters, performers, people persons or perfectionists. Each of these types can be difficult, but in different ways. The approach also depends on whether the person is passive or aggressive.

Fortunately there are proven strategies you can use in dealing with unproductive behavior. Your specific response depends on their work style and whether they are passive or aggressive types. Here are specific ways to deal with the most common types of difficult people.

■ The Bully

These people are aggressive taskmasters, and use intimidation to get their own way. Bullies are tough to deal with because they attack knowing most people avoid confrontation. For example, if a bullying reporter doesn't like a story assignment, he marches across the newsroom, stands over the assignment editor and loudly explains that this is the stupidest story he's ever been assigned. The desk person cowers and tells the reporter she'll find them a better story. Here are some tips for coping with the office bully:

Stand your ground but do not get in a confrontation. Bullies enjoy confrontation because they are good at it and can win.

Stand your ground by standing up, if they are standing, and facing the bully. Make eye contact. Stay calm and attempt to explain the situation without being defensive. When they interrupt you, use their name, calmly telling them they are interrupting. "John, you are interrupting me. Here's why we want you to do this story. John, you are interrupting me again. Let me explain that this is an important story and you're the right person. John, you are interrupting me again." This may go on for some time. You might have to go through this drill more than once until the bully understands you won't be bullied.

Don't use body language or gestures that look threatening. The appearance of a threat will only encourage the bully to keep up the battle. Stay in command of your emotions. The bully wins if you lose your temper or break down in tears.

Once you've demonstrated you can't be intimidated, a bully will often treat you with respect and become a friend. Admittedly, it's tough to cope with intimidation, but you've got to learn how if you want to be a power producer.

■ The Put-down Artist

There are two types of put-down artists. The most dangerous is the aggressive personality who uses put-downs to intimidate others. They try to control a situation by making comments putting down others and their ideas. These are normally task-oriented people who want to get their own way but don't like confrontation. They have a passive aggressive personality. For example, a producer has a story idea and brings it up in the story meeting only to be hit with a put-down. "Gee, Stephanie, I see you're getting your hard-hitting investigative ideas from *Cosmo* again." Everyone laughs and the producer shuts up for the rest of the meeting.

The second type of put-down artist is less dangerous. These personalities look for recognition and acceptance. They enjoy the dark humor found in the newsroom. The major problem with this type of humor is it hurts others. This doesn't build teamwork. Also, humor that goes beyond good taste can border on sexual harassment. It can create what is called a hostile work environment. Here's how to cope with this work type:

You've got to call the put-down artists' bluff. Most people in the newsroom don't like put-downs anymore than you do, but laugh because they want to be accepted. Don't let people get away with cheap shots. Like bullies, they operate in the safety of knowing that most people don't like confrontation. Respond with a line like, "What did you mean by that comment?" Or, "Were you making fun of the story idea?"

It may well take more than one confrontation to stop the put-down artist, but you have to keep at it. If someone doesn't stop, then you may have to set up a meeting to tell him that you don't appreciate put-downs. He may verbally attack you so you will have to respond just as you would respond to a bully.

One of the problems with the put-down artist is that he can go underground after being exposed in public. What do you do if you hear someone is putting you down behind your back? Ask the person who told you about the backstabbing if you can use his or her name, then meet privately with the put-down artist. Don't let him intimidate you. If it still doesn't stop, take it to your boss and, if necessary, the news director. Insist they deal with the problem because this behavior can poison a newsroom.

■ The Bomb

It's common in television news to have people explode in the newsroom, the control room or on the set. It's also unproductive and disruptive. The human bomb (taskmaster and performer, aggressive) leaves all kinds of debris behind and can poison the environment for years.

For example, you're calmly telling the news director why you don't think it's a good idea to run the special sweeps series on heavy metal rock bands in your early newscast when the news director suddenly goes ballistic. He's screaming at you in the most unflattering terms and everyone in the office dives for cover. What set him off? It can be all kinds of reasons, some not even related to work. His car broke down this morning or the GM is on him about the overtime budget. You're the last straw.

Afterward, the bomb person normally feels terrible and sorry for blowing up. Unfortunately, there is little he can do in the way of damage control. However, if you can keep your wits about you during the explosion, you may be able to lessen the damage. Some tips for coping with this type of person:

The best way to cope is to try to contain it quickly. At the same time, you don't want to make the situation worse by allowing it to become a screaming match. At first you'll be stunned, but as you get your emotions under control, try to interrupt the person. Use his name calmly but with force.

If this doesn't get his attention, then try to call a break. Buy him time to cool down and get his emotions under control. Then as quickly as possible, resume the discussion. Probe with open-ended questions, looking for the cause. Explosions often happen because people think that they are being ignored or even deliberately thwarted. Calmly help him understand you share his concern.

■ The Whiner

Every newsroom has whiners. These people think there is a perfect newsroom someplace, despite all evidence to the contrary. Whiners see lots of problems and lots of blame but have few practical solutions. These are life's victims, the powerless. The problem for you as a team leader is the whiner's ability to pull down morale and get teammates focused on the wrong problems. Whiners are also masters of the blame game. "So and so can never get anything right" is a typical whiner complaint based on a single mistake. However, don't be confused between people who have a legitimate complaint and whiners who just like to gripe.

Whining takes place away from newsroom managers. Whining happens in the news cars, during the overnight shift and in the smoking area. Most of this griping is unproductive and annoying but it can require a response if it's getting in the way of a successful newscast. Here are tips for coping with whiners:

Although painful, the first step with a whiner is to hear him out. Listen to what he says and how he says it. Don't agree with the whiner; that just keeps him going. Don't argue or explain as he might start arguing, ending any hope of a productive conversation.

As you listen, take notes and ask questions to make sure you understand the point. Once you think you understand the complaint, then use more questions to get specifics. Many whiners deal in broad generalities and are vague about details. Whiners also tend to exaggerate, making a single incident far too important. If whiners don't have the facts then urge them to go out and get more information. Ask them to get back to you with real data.

Next, shift the conversation to finding a solution to the complaint. Don't try to solve the problem for him. If it really is important, he'll find a way to deal with the issue. If not, the whiner will stop complaining, at least around you.

Sometimes you may need to bring a whiner back to reality. There are limits on what can be done. If a desk assistant is complaining about her workload, the news director can't add more production assistants to the payroll if the budget is tight.

Whiners often feel powerless and not in control. Find an important goal he can work toward. Get the whiner focused on solutions and a better future. A little recognition for good work will help also.

When a whiner persists in whining then you have to let him know you really aren't interested unless he has answers and solutions for his complaints. Sometimes you just have to cut him off and get back to work on something more productive, like creating a newscast.

■ The "No" Person

Negative people abound in television newsrooms. No people don't want to stick out their necks to try something new or to take a risk with a new production idea. Failure might reflect badly on them. Sometimes, they're negative because they don't like news; it's sloppy and challenging when the news changes or something breaks. News production is threatening to perfectionists.

Directors who tell you something can't be done may actually be avoiding a potential mistake. She doesn't want to get yelled at by her boss, the production manager. On the other hand, she also may be protecting a technician she isn't confident can do what you want. Negative people aren't bad. They're locked into a careful way of doing things. They fear risk. Here's how to cope with this personality type:

It takes perseverance to bring a no person around to thinking creatively. At one time most people got in the business because it was exciting and challenging, but possibly poor management and negative feedback has taken that passion out of them. Restore that passion; focus them on accomplishment, reward and recognition if they can get the job done successfully.

Pushing a no person to do something only makes them dig in more. So shift into a fact-finding mode. Ask specific questions to get at the heart of the problem. Why can't something be done? What are the specific obstacles? This is tough to do on deadline but you can't give up trying to get the no person out of his posture.

■ The Know-it-all

The know-it-all is more than willing to tell you and everyone else how to do your job. He learned the television news business long ago and you don't know anything. When you want to try something new or creative, these are the people who say, "We've never done it that way" or "We tried that once but it didn't work."

Know-it-alls are threatened by change. They want to get the job done and don't want any changes from you, the new young producer. They consider you dangerous because you might get in the way of getting the newscast on the air safely. How do you deal with the know-it-all?

As with so many of these difficult people you need to find the specifics. Why can't something be done differently? Like the "no people," use patience and careful questions to get the facts. All the while, treat the know-it-all with honest respect. In fact, as someone who knows the station's systems, the know-it-all can really become a valuable resource for you. He can tell you why something is included in your newscast even when you think it's a bad idea. He has the history, you don't.

When trying to get a know-it-all to change his mind, do so carefully. Don't just hit him with a new idea. Take time to set up the idea. Give him some background, reasons and time to digest the concept.

■ The "Maybe" and "Yes" People

These two similar types of difficult people want to please and to avoid confrontation. The yes people tell you they'll do something but don't, while the maybe people won't commit to giving you an answer one way or the other. Both are frustrating. An example is the reporter who tells you that her story will be done in time for your show when that's just not possible. On the other hand, the indecisive tape editor isn't sure if it will get done or not, equally annoying. Some of these difficult people use indecision to cope because they've been punished in the past for being honest. These people are difficult because you can't trust them. You may like them, many are amiable, but a newsroom is not a place people come together to have a nice time. People in television are part of a process with tough deadlines. Here are tips for coping with this type of worker:

Work first on your relationship with these types. Take time to build their trust. This takes clear agreement on decisions and on deadlines.

With a yes person you want to ask questions to test his willingness to agree. Has he thought through the situation? What other factors does he face that might get in the way of getting the job done?

In working with both types, be sure to keep building trust so they will feel free to be honest with you, to say no when appropriate.

■ The "Nothing" Person

These are people who are so passive that they avoid dealing with problems and confrontation. They are quiet and reluctant to respond to specific requests or questions. Their first impulse is to hide and avoid the problem. Frankly, you don't deal with this type of person in the newsroom often. Unfortunately, some become angry and difficult to work with. Some technical people fall into this category. They can sometimes sabotage a newscast by not warning anyone about a potential problem. Not helpful. How does a manager cope with this type of person?

The best way to cope is to demonstrate you understand their concerns about doing things right. Again, use questions to find their concerns and keep things comfortable and non-threatening. At the first sign of trouble they'll go into their shells. Share with them your team's goals and explain how the news process can be done more carefully in the future with their help.

Dealing with Team Conflict

While people can be difficult as individuals, differences within a team can also be difficult. Conflict isn't necessarily bad. Even though most producers avoid conflict and find it threatening, it's actually something to be encouraged. Conflict helps bring to light issues that get in the way of creating a better newscast. Don't avoid conflict but learn to deal with team differences as part of your job.

The reasons behind conflict. There are four basic reasons why you have to deal with conflict.

■ **Different work types.** You've just read about all the different work styles people bring to the team and how people can be difficult. Even on the best of teams these work styles are going to clash. Be prepared and be understanding. Deal with these conflicts. Don't avoid them or they become more frequent and volatile.

■ **Unrealistic expectations.** Some team members develop unrealistic expectations. If your newscast doesn't enjoy the ratings everyone wants, some team members think the ratings can be turned around quickly. They get discouraged and difficult when the ratings don't improve quickly. A team leader helps them understand and develop realistic, achievable short-term goals.

■ **Lack of communication.** Clear and open communication is at the heart of teamwork. Unfortunately, such communication is not always possible in the news process. Working at a hectic pace against deadlines, producers don't stop long enough to make sure they've communicated properly. As you learned in the last chapter, a power producer must use listening and questioning skills to have a two-way conversation.

■ **Confusion over who does what.** Conflict also results when there isn't a clear definition of roles and responsibilities. When the person responsible for getting a job done isn't clear about her duties then the news process breaks down. You can go to the blame mode but a power producer will make sure team members know their specific roles.

How to avoid conflict. Think about the problems you've already experienced in producing. Most of the problems can be traced to indecision on your part, a failure to communicate clearly or a failure to anticipate the work types of different team members. As a power producer, you need to sit down with the team and try to find out what actually caused the conflict. As you know, you need to look for the deeper cause of a breakdown. There are ways to analyze process breakdowns such as a flowchart or a cause-and-effect diagram. Both tools, used with brainstorming, allow a team to isolate each step in a process until the real problems become apparent. This is also a good time to keep asking why over and over until you peel back the issue to its core. When you force a compromise you'll probably solve the immediate conflict, but only temporarily.

> **TIP**
> **GETTING ALONG**
>
>
>
> When dealing with difficult people always remember that you are trying to cope and change the way in which they work with you and your team. This is about coping in the workplace, getting the job done. We are not trying to change someone's basic beliefs and work style. You don't have the skills or the time.

If the needs of all parties aren't met, your quick compromise is going to break down just as soon as there is a new problem. Look for a final, win-win resolution.

Resolving team conflict. Going for a win-win solution is the best way to resolve a conflict. Win-win means finding a solution that meets the needs of everyone involved. Bring those involved together, use an open discussion, hear out each party and then try to find a solution that meets the needs of each. Get each person to explain what he or she thinks is going on. Use questions to test their assumptions. Tell them they can't refer to another person but only to what they believe happened. No one involved can be allowed to make judgmental statements or personal accusations.

When you've succeeded in mastering how to coach your team and deal with difficult people, you'll find yourself far along the road to being a power producer. To help you succeed, Resources for Producers at the back of the book includes a list of books on dealing with difficult people and work types.

News ratings and research can mean life or death to a producer's career. In the next chapter discover how to read those mysterious Nielsen ratings and see how news research can build a more successful newscast.

Chapter 14 — Role Six: Researcher

Ratings & Research

In This Chapter:

- Why Ratings Are Important
- How Nielsen Works
- How Are the Numbers Collected?
- What Ratings Mean to Producers
- The Sweeps Rules
- Know Your Viewers
- Types of Research

Chapter 14: Ratings & Research

"The ratings are critical because they determine advertising revenue, the way stations make money."

Every few months, you and your colleagues find yourselves battling your way through yet another Nielsen sweeps month. For a producer, the sweeps border on stress overload. You aren't sure what series you will air next week because it isn't even shot yet. Of course, you've lost your reporter and photographer for the newscast because they're working on a special report for a different show. Plus, the promotion director wants you to do a report in conjunction with a prime-time movie on a subject completely without redeeming news value. Everything about the sweeps contributes to your worry and anxiety.

Your tension lasts until the Nielsen book hits the newsroom two or three weeks after the month ends. With a ratings win you get champagne poured by the news director. With a defeat, you may not even get a clear explanation of what the book reported! Instead, there are closed-door meetings and some people start looking for jobs, casualties of ratings combat.

Nielsen ratings. In the television wars, Nielsen Media Research keeps score both locally and nationally. The local measurement service is called the Nielsen Station Index or NSI. A producer absolutely must know how Nielsen arrives at that score, the ratings. You need to know how Nielsen works because its methodology actually dictates how you produce your newscast. The ability to read, interpret and massage the Nielsen survey can be the difference between victory and defeat.

Nielsen ratings are based on statistical sampling, the same techniques used in audience research. While Nielsen is measuring the size and makeup of your audience, your station is doing research to find out what the audience thinks about your newscast. The object of audience research is to find out how to win more viewers during the sweeps.

Why Ratings Are Important
There's a lot more at stake in the ratings wars than the public, and even some news producers, may realize. The public thinks Nielsen measures the popularity of television programs. They see a weekly list of top-rated network programs and read newspaper articles about which local newscast is number one. However, the Nielsen ratings are about far more than who is number one. The ratings are critical because they determine advertising revenue, the way stations make money.

Advertisers buy time in your newscast to reach potential customers. They want to know exactly how many people watch your newscast. What advertisers need is a way to measure your circulation. Newspapers measure circulation based on counting the newspapers printed and sold. You can't do that in television, so Nielsen measures the size of the audience using a statistical sample. Nielsen research provides advertisers with a statistical snapshot of circulation, broken down into ratings, shares and demographics.

How Nielsen Works
To understand what the ratings say about your newscast, you need to know how Nielsen collects the information. And to understand that process you also have to learn some unique terms, found only in broadcast ratings reports. Here are the key terms and how ratings are collected.

Designated Market Area. The Nielsens start with the Designated Market Area (DMA). This is the region on which the viewing sample is based and where your audience lives. The DMA is made up of a cluster of counties in which the majority of television households watch the stations from a Metropolitan Statistical Area (MSA). Each year, Nielsen decides which county goes to which market based on viewership. Every county

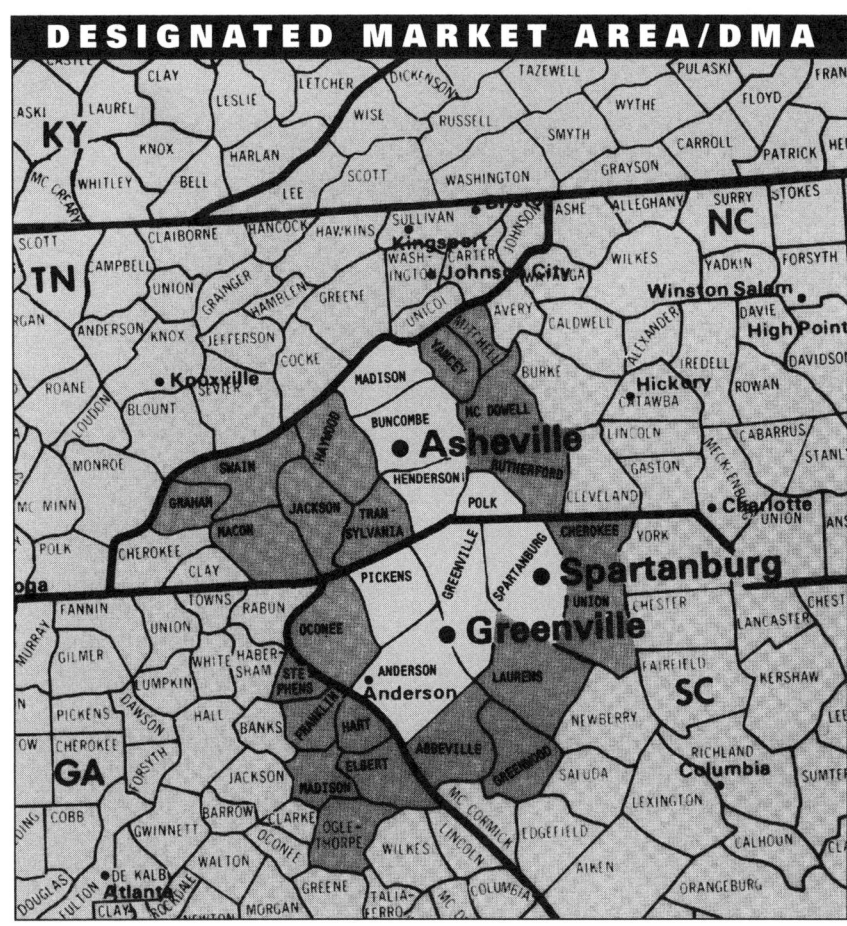

DESIGNATED MARKET AREA/DMA

in the nation is assigned to one DMA. You'll find a map of the counties in your DMA on the inside front cover of the Nielsen book.

Pictured above is the DMA map for the 35th largest market, Greenville-Spartanburg, SC-Asheville, NC-Anderson, SC. Covering two states, this is one of the more complicated hyphenated markets. The counties in white are the MSA while the darker counties are the DMA. The first four pages of a ratings book provide excellent and valuable material on the makeup of your market.

Metropolitan Statistical Area. Called the metro, this is the central city or cities of the DMA and is actually defined by the federal government. You also find metro viewership measured in the ratings book. These ratings and shares can be helpful to you as a producer. They can tell you if your newscast is doing better with city dwellers or with viewers in more suburban or rural counties.

Television Households. Ratings (RTG) and shares (SHR) are usually stated in terms of television households (HH), or TVHH. There are also ratings and shares for many different demographics, such as men 18-34 or adults 50 plus.

Ratings. A ratings point is the primary means for expressing circulation. A ratings point represents 1 percent of the total television households in your DMA. To give you an example, if there are 250,000 television households in your market, then one rating point represents 2,500 television households. If a newscast has a rating of 10, 25,000 households are viewing it. Ratings tell you how many television households are watching your newscast from the total television households in your market.

Share. The other way Nielsen defines your audience is the share. This is the percentage of the television households where people actually have their sets on and are watching your newscast during each quarter hour. Shares tell you how well you are doing in drawing viewers.

Cost Per Point. There's a direct relationship between ratings and what your station can charge for commercials in your newscast. Advertisers negotiate to pay a specific amount for each ratings point, called cost per point (CPP). A good Nielsen book, with better ratings than the last sweeps, translates into more sales revenue for your station. In larger markets an additional ratings point can be worth millions of dollars in added revenue. This is why the sweeps are so serious!

Demo points. However, television sales get even more

TIP
RATINGS BEFORE SHARE

It is standard practice in television to refer to ratings first and then shares: "We got a 6-20." This means a 6 rating for that program with a 20 share. Ratings will always be lower than shares.

TIP
RATINGS, SHARES AND THE COMPETITION

Ratings and shares do different jobs when you're trying to figure out if you are winning or losing viewers from book to book. Ratings should be compared to previous books in the same sweeps periods, such as November ratings to November ratings. Outside factors like weather and lifestyle cause swings in the size of the audience from book to book. For instance, there are more households using television (HUTs) in the February book than the July book because of weather and vacations. However, audience share is valuable as a way of knowing whether you are gaining or losing audience from book to book. Share measures your performance with those actually viewing. It's one indication of how well you're doing in competition with other channels, despite outside factors.

TIP
THE BOOK BREAKOUT

Your station management should put out a memo on the book and hold a meeting to explain what happened. However, if you really want to get heavily into the Nielsens, to understand exactly what the book says, ask if you can sit in when the sales staff does its book breakout analysis of your newscast.

---

complicated. Advertisers actually buy time in your newscast based on demographic ratings. Nielsen reports are broken down into different demographic categories, such as sex and age. A demo point is a rating point based on 1 percent of all the people in the market in a demographic group. The most requested demographic rating in local television is women aged 25-54, followed by adults 25-54. For example, auto dealers are the most important advertisers in local television news precisely because newscasts reach the dealers' customers, adults 25-54.

Those newspaper articles on your ratings seldom tell the complete story because they seldom report the demographic battle. The demographic ratings are critical from a business viewpoint because they determine how well a station will do in sales. Given the importance of demographics, your news director may ask you to tailor your teases, promos and even stories to viewers of a certain sex or age. This isn't always sound journalism, but one way the Nielsens and sales can influence your newscast.

How Are the Numbers Collected?

Once you understand the basics of DMA, ratings and share, you need to know how Nielsen collects the numbers. There are two different methods. As this handbook is being written, Nielsen is measuring the 46 largest local television markets using meters.

In addition, in all of the 210 markets, Nielsen uses paper diaries to gather demographic viewing data.

Meters. Nielsen has meters in each of these top 46 DMAs and is adding about four new metered markets each year. The company places 400 or more meters in each market. These boxes are hooked up to viewers' television sets. They read when the sets are on and which channels they're tuned to during each quarter hour.

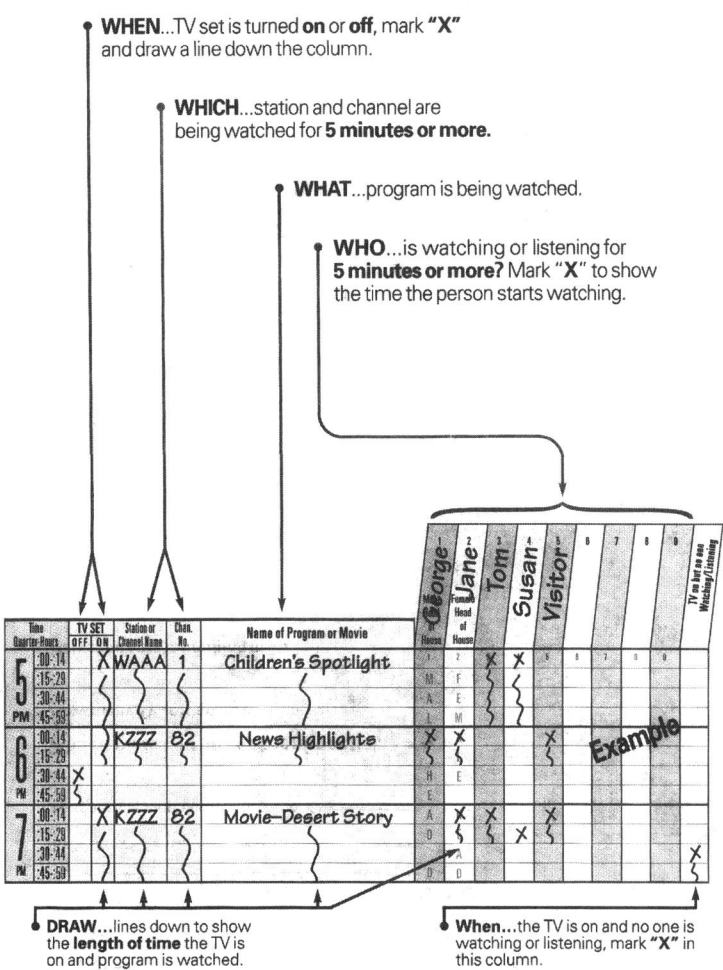

The overnights. Using telephone lines, the data from these local meters is collected daily by Nielsen's computers in Dunedin, FL, and processed overnight. Metered market stations then access the Nielsen computers every morning to download the previous day's ratings. These are the overnights, which are copied and distributed each morning through the station to anxious managers.

Reading overnight ratings reports can cost you your eyesight. The left column is the time in 15-minute increments. In the right columns are the ratings and shares by quarter hour. In the center of each station column are the program titles and the ratings and shares for that program.

Diaries and sweeps. All stations, at least four months a year, are measured by paper diaries. Diary sweeps are conducted in all markets during February, May, July and November. There are other sweeps months in the largest markets, in March, October and January. Each sweeps month lasts exactly four weeks. Each week of the sweeps, starting on a Thursday, a new set of households records their viewing.

A page in the diary shows viewers how to fill out the pages. You can see why call letters, channel numbers and program name are so important.

The sample. Nielsen calls a random sample of the public to find 200 households willing to fill out diaries for a week. Each quarter hour, viewers write in the diaries the station and program they are watching by call letters, channel number and program name.

The demos. The value of diaries is in their demographic data. Every viewer is asked for information such as age, sex, race, location and employment. The diary also requests information like the number of television sets and video recorders in the house.

The local ratings book. After the sweeps are over, Nielsen Media collects and sorts this data. In Florida, a person called a diary editor reads each diary and enters the data in Nielsen's computer. Then the company issues the local ratings book, the Viewers in Profile (VIP). The book arrives roughly 15 days after the sweeps period ends. The news director and perhaps some of the news managers get copies. Borrow one and spend time going through the book carefully.

When you first look at a local ratings book, take time to study all the information and try to absorb what the numbers tell you. Look for things like metro ratings and share, demographic data and how your newscast did each day. This can be helpful in learning your market and your audience. The data also tells you a good deal about how your audience flows through and around your newscast. For instance, if your newscast has a weak lead-in program but attracts new viewers, you can take comfort that people are actually tuning in to your news.

Your station can also order special reports from Nielsen Media, for an extra fee. These reports include flow studies that show where viewers tune from lead-in and lead-out programs and where they tune even during your newscasts. Flow studies help you know what stories to promote and tease, particularly before your news. Another special report available in certain markets reports the viewing of specific audiences like African-Americans or Hispanics.

Another valuable Nielsen report provides information on the meter sample panel. It tells you where the meters are located by zip code, along with viewer statistics like income, education and occupation. Because of the meter panel, your news director may ask you to cover stories from those zip codes.

What Ratings Mean to Producers

How Nielsen Media collects the ratings, with both meters and diaries, makes a difference for producers. For instance, in filling out a diary, viewers must correctly write down two of the three criteria—channel, call letters or program name—for a

**WARNING!
DON'T OVER-REACT TO OVERNIGHTS**

One of the problems with overnights is that producers and everyone else in the newsroom tend to overreact. After a bad day, producers start fretting over story placement, second-guessing themselves. Of course, after a good day they can also be overconfident! But station and newscast success is based on long-term trends and averages. The most important thing is that the newscast is consistently getting better and better.

**TIP
KEEP A LOG**

During the sweeps, keep a daily log of special reports, the weather, breaking news and anything else that could influence a newscast. When going back over the book day by day, this log helps you know what worked and what didn't.

station to get credit for that viewer. This is the reason the channel number and station logo appear as a bug on the screen and why you put the channel number and newscast name on all supers.

The 5-minute rule. One critical rule for producers in metered markets is the 5-minute rule. To get credit for viewership your newscast has to be viewed, although not continuously, for at least five minutes in each quarter hour. Talk about a producing challenge! You've got to hold that crazed viewer with the clicker for five minutes. And this Nielsen rule also dictates you build in 5 strong minutes in your second quarter hour.

Power producers use a variety of techniques to make sure they keep the audience engaged for 5 minutes or more.

■ Format the program to have 5 minutes of strong content starting each quarter hour.

■ Lengthen weather and add additional news stories to the third block to make it a strong 5 minutes.

■ Use seamless breaks in and out of the newscast.

■ Place promotable, interesting stories in the second quarter hour.

■ Use teases throughout.

■ Always tease the next story after the break. This means you have to place a promotable story as the block lead.

■ Use teases and a strong closer to pull viewers across the sports segment or leave sports to the end.

■ When appropriate, tailor your teases and special reports to your lead-in or lead-out programming.

The Sweeps Rules

You and your news department must actively plan for each sweeps month. This means you need to know the various rules Nielsen Media uses to keep sweeps ratings as accurate as possible. Power producers take advantage of the rules without breaking them. Here are five ideas to keep in mind as you face a sweeps month.

Sweeps planning. Successful newsrooms plan sweeps months well in advance. Their plan includes a specific timetable for each news series, special report or special event opportunity in the month. You need to be included because as a team leader it's your job to make sure everyone on your newscast team understands the plan and his or her role.

Metered market planning. If anything, sweeps in metered markets are more intense than in diary markets. Stations convene a team to look at each day of the book, including the different network programs, to develop and execute a sweeps game plan. As a producer, you will be directly involved as this team adjusts your station's marketing and promotion for special reports and events.

Rounding up. Metered stations try to use another Nielsen rule. Ratings are first reported to the nearest 10th, but Nielsen rounds up the ratings numbers for the VIP report. A station's sweeps team will track which newscasts have a chance to round up to a higher rating and maybe win the time period. They then try to boost that rating. As a producer, you'll suddenly be assigned a special report and be given additional advertising support for your newscast, or suffer the reverse, a loss of resources.

Stunts. In sweeps, your station can do other things to take advantage of the rules. These are so-called stunts. These aren't the sort of decisions you make as a producer, but stunts certainly affect your newscast. For example, Nielsen Media allows stations to take special programs out of the regular program averages. So, faced with strong competition, stations do things like start the newscast early and give it a new name. Or they shorten the news program on a given night when it looks like the network will give you a weak lead-in. For

---

TIP — THE DMA LIST

You can find the rank order of all markets in a number of locations on the web, including UltimateTV.com. The *Broadcasting & Cable Yearbook*, found in many libraries, lists the DMAs and has maps of the counties with population and station data on each market. Audience Research & Development's *Little Black Book* and the National Association of Television Program Executives (NATPE) *Station Guide* both list the markets by size and provide station telephone numbers. The NATPE guide is more complete. You can learn how to order these guides in the Resources for Producers appendix at the end of the handbook.

TIP — DIARY STRATEGY

It's good policy, even if you aren't in a metered market, to produce so that the audience stays tuned as long as possible. Always follow the 5-minute rule in producing. Also, this just might help viewers remember which station they watched for news. A memorable newscast is more likely to be recorded correctly in a diary.

instance, the night of the final Seinfeld episode on NBC, the ABC stations started their newscasts early to take the rating for that night out of the book.

Know Your Viewers

Ultimately, the most powerful tool stations and channels have to improve their Nielsen numbers is audience research. Audience research uses a statistical sample to find out what the viewers think of your anchors, the news content and dozens of other issues that affect the Nielsen ratings. It's necessary that you not only understand the Nielsen numbers but also how to use audience research.

Before you got involved in television news you knew the name Nielsen. However, few outside television have heard of Frank N. Magid and Associates, Audience Research & Development, Broadcast Image Group, or any of the other audience research and television news-consulting firms. These and others conduct research for stations. They then use the results to make recommendations about how to improve the news broadcasts. As a producer, you'll probably deal with consultants and their research during one of their station visits.

You can't produce a good newscast without knowing what viewers think. The most effective way to find out what they think is through marketing research. Today, most stations or networks do extensive research. This research tells the station about all kinds of different issues. Research helps you understand which stories are important to viewers and how your newscasts are doing in comparison to other news broadcasts in your market. It also tells about viewing habits and how well your news appeals to different demographic groups.

Talent. Because popular talent is a key to ratings success, the most important part of any research is the talent question. Your station has to know how your news anchors, weathercasters and sportscasters stack up against the competition. Are they winning new viewers or barely hanging on to your current fans? The only way to properly answer talent questions is through statistical research.

The Q score. How viewers perceive your news talent is found in the Q score, or by some similar ranking. This score tries to define talent attributes like familiarity, believability, and, ultimately, likeability. A research study will then rank all the major talent in your market by their scores. When station managers or news directors see an anchor whose Q score is getting better or is high after only a short time in the market, then you can expect to see that person given more on-air responsibility in your newscast. This is one way research has a direct impact on you and your newscast.

Content. Research also measures content and newscast elements. Viewers are asked to rank common topics like crime, education, politics and medicine. You also find yourself making different news judgments based on what the research says about your viewers' news needs. As you know, issues your viewers find significant, like medicine and education, often become franchises.

Competition. Another part of most audience studies looks at the competitive situation. Do people like your newscast more now than last year? How is your station doing relative to the competition over time? How does that newscast appeal to certain target demographic groups? The answer to these questions lets you and news management know if you're winning a new audience. This type of information can identify viewing trends well in advance of the Nielsen ratings. It also gives news management data

---

TIP
TALENT DECISIONS

When you arrive in a new market, you may wonder why your station keeps bad anchors on the air. The answer is that these anchors have a bond with the audience that has built up over the years. Talent decisions, particularly firing or demoting an anchor, aren't made on gut instinct. Smart general managers and news directors rely on research to help make the call.

WARNING! USE CAUTION

You and your newsroom need to use care in trying to influence the sweeps numbers. For instance, if your station tries to spike the ratings book and runs a contest, like giving away money during your newscast, Nielsen alerts advertisers. A special warning notice goes in the front of the local ratings book telling advertisers that a station held a contest to influence the ratings. Sometimes management doesn't care and you find yourself running a contest within your news anyway. If you are employed in the television industry, you are not allowed to participate in Nielsen samples. If Nielsen Media contacts you to complete a diary, explain that you work for a television station or a cable channel. Don't just say no and hang up.

needed to make adjustments in the station's news strategy.

Types of Research

Audience research evolved from marketing research and still uses the same research methods to find out what viewers think. Today, there are two primary forms of news audience research.

Focus groups. To get in-depth comments from selected viewers and to uncover opportunities or threats, researchers often use focus groups. A focus group is a panel of viewers, a dozen or so, who come to a facility where they spend several hours answering questions about local news. The moderator uses questions to keep the group on the subject and to get the best information. Station management, including producers, can watch from behind a one-way mirror, but sessions are also taped. Focus groups yield information on issues that news management needs to address. However, because of the small sample, focus groups aren't considered scientific.

There's a variation on focus groups in which the moderator asks the group to watch a newscast and record their reactions on a hand-held dial. Panelists turn it higher if they really like some aspect of the newscast or down if they don't like something. These sessions give strong feedback on specific parts of your newscast, virtually second to second. An interesting test is to take producers from your station and compare their reactions to the newscast with those of the viewers. It can be radically different!

Telephone surveys. Most stations rely on more statistically accurate telephone surveys to get a picture of the broader market. Telephone surveys are considered better research because of the larger sample. To make surveys more useful, the station can target a specific, key demographic group. Unfortunately, because of the increase in telephone marketing, researchers find that fewer people are willing to take the 20 or more minutes needed to answer a telephone questionnaire.

Tracking studies. Larger stations can afford to keep asking a battery of standard questions in periodic telephone surveys over time. This allows them to see what is working and what isn't. This ongoing research is called a tracking study since it tracks performance trends.

When a study is completed, your news consultants write a report, often three thick volumes of data. They then deliver the results to station and news department management using an elaborate PowerPoint presentation. Your consultants will make recommendations to management on talent development and on content issues. They also suggest ways to improve station marketing and promotion. Producers are often included in these presentations. This is an opportunity for you to ask questions and get the consultants' interpretation of the results in person.

Research is now part of everyday life in television and television news. As a producer, you're deeply dependent on research. For one thing, Nielsen research tells you whether you are winning or losing the television news wars. Audience research helps determine essential elements of your newscast, like talent, franchises and content. However, power producers don't allow research to substitute for good sense and knowledge based on years of professional development.

Ahead, in the next chapter, you dive into law and ethics, another power producer role that also requires good sense and knowledge. It's another role you must master.

TIP — ANCHOR ALERT

Be aware that talent research results are the most sensitive part of any study. They aren't shared with you or the news staff for both personal and competitive reasons. However, some news directors do share Q score data personally with talent. Inevitably the anchors and other talent find out when a news research study is underway. Either the anchors become more involved in the newscast or they get more difficult and prickly. Power producers keep a steady hand on their newscasts when anchors go into consultant "angst" mode.

Interview: Television News Consultant

Desiree Newhart Hill
*Senior Account Executive
Audience Research & Development
Dallas*

Desiree Hill is AR&D's strategic specialist on newscast producing. She has 19 years of broadcast news experience. Prior to joining AR&D in 1996, Desiree was executive producer at KWTV in Oklahoma City. She also worked in Oklahoma City at KOCO-TV as a producer and then executive producer. She produced at KOLR-TV in Springfield, MO, and KHBS-TV in Fort Smith, AR. She began her broadcasting career at KHBS in production jobs including directing, camera operator, tape editing, and eventually reporting.

What does a young news producer need to know about audience research?

My first thought is to ask the news director to share the information. A lot of the stations we work with hold this information so close to the vest nobody benefits. News directors often won't share information because they feel it is going to get across the street and wind up in the hands of the competition.

Once the information is shared, I recommend that entry-level and relatively inexperienced producers ask questions if they don't understand some aspect of the plan or if it doesn't make sense. For instance, the news director may say the station is going to target one geographic area. A lot of young people in the business will say, "Well, what about the rest of our viewing area?" That's not what they learned in journalism school.

Then the other point is to ask, "What can I do to help?" For instance, if your station is perceived as dull and boring in the research, the news director might want to update the graphics. Maybe the news director would be thrilled, especially in a small market, if they could delegate some of the project to a producer.

Also, when you have your target or goal, don't forget it. For instance, I just came off a research project and we have four major goals. What I would like is a card at each producer's and reporter's computer outlining the four targets: one, two, three, four. Having been a producer, I love this idea. When you get writer's block when you're writing a tease, glance at that card and you know whom you are talking to. You are talking to one person. You don't have to make this tease work for every demographic.

Some stations do pictures of target viewers. For instance, in south Texas, the picture of your target viewer might be of an Hispanic woman holding a baby. When you go to the morning meeting, when you format the newscast, and when you start to write, you've got this picture in mind. Yes, it does exclude certain viewers, but you have to win a segment of the audience in order to build any kind of platform. I think young producers have to learn that in today's competitive environment we can't wrap our arms around every single viewer.

A strategic problem with young producers, and young people in general, is that they want to produce the shows for themselves and people like them. They must realize they aren't like the viewers. What the research does is help identify audience segments. Because the producers are different from the audience it's hard for them to put themselves in the viewers' minds.

Another thing that should happen is to share the research results with the directors. Producers have a love-hate relationship with their directors. For instance, at a station where I just did research, we had conversations about the directors. We were going to update the graphic look and add mini-digests. The producers' reaction was that the production department can't do it, that they'll hate it. Be proactive; suggest the directors be brought in to share the research. Explain the problem areas and the goals. You've got to get buy-in from the directors. If it comes from on high, they are probably going to resist. Ask them, "What do you think we can do to improve our graphics and add mini-digests?" The directors are probably going to come up with two or three ideas that you are going to include. Guess who's going to be willing to work harder?

Should producers be included when consultants come to do their report and make recommendations?

Usually what we do, as consultants, is to present the research and then strategize. For the producers' sake, it's good to have almost everything buttoned down before they get involved. Now when I was a producer I probably would have wanted to help strategize. Frankly, I didn't have enough information. But when the strategy is set that's when producers get involved. They can throw out ideas like doing a "Dateline"-style timeline and go after the baby-boomers. Those kinds of ideas can come from producers.

I also think there has to be follow-up. The strategy has to be monitored and measured. For instance, in one market we are going after a geographic area. What makes it difficult is some of the people on the staff think we are ignoring a big city in the area. For a lot of reasons we are. Two television stations are in that city and we aren't. We are never going to win in that city, so we need to win in our own territory. What we need to monitor and measure are how many stories we do from that target geographic area every day. So from the morning meeting on, the strategy is reinforced and there's no avoiding it. There's a saying that what gets measured, gets done.

Chapter 15

Role Seven: Lawyer/Ethicist

The Law, Ethics & Your Newscast

In This Chapter:

- The Law and the Producer
- Privacy Law
- Your Ethical Foundation
- News Smarts

Chapter 15:
The Law, Ethics & Your Newscast

"To avoid a libel judgment against you, the best defense is that the story is accurate and true."

The phone rings just as you arrive back at your desk after the newscast. You dump your script on the desk and pick up the phone. The caller is a furious viewer, so angry he barely makes sense. He demands an immediate retraction. His complaint involves a story you just ran on an increase in sexually transmitted diseases. He says he was shown in the report. You're not sure what his complaint is all about—all you had done was ask an intern to pull some file tape to use in a 20-second voice over. How big a problem can that create? Actually, it could cause a major problem. It could cost your station a good deal of money, and you your job. It happened at one station, it could happen to you.

Unfortunately, some producers think legal issues involve the news director and station lawyers, anyone else but them. Actually, you are responsible. You could find yourself in a difficult situation if you don't have a solid grounding in both the laws governing journalism and the ethical standards of television news. The first section of this chapter gives you a basic knowledge of libel and privacy laws. Then, you'll learn about the major ethical issues you'll face and get the news smarts you'll need to deal with those issues.

The Law and the Producer
Federal and state laws have a major say in how you do your job. The laws you have to worry about are those concerned with libel and privacy. To master the legal side of producing, you need to know the basics of libel law.

How do you libel someone? Libel in a news story is to damage or defame a person, group or institution's reputation or character by saying something about them that's not true and doing it with malice. It's libel if written but slander if spoken, although in television news you're considered to have libeled someone in most states because the script is printed.

What constitutes libel? Under the law, the following elements must be present to constitute the potential for a successful libel suit.

■ The statement needs to be published. This means printed in a newspaper or broadcast on a television program.
■ The person who charges you with libel must be identified although this does not mean he or she is actually named. If friends or associates can identify the individual or group from the story, you've still got a problem.
■ The statement or information must damage that person's reputation.
■ The person suing has to prove that he or she was harmed by the libel.
■ The statement or information must be false.
■ The plaintiff must show that the channel or station demonstrated negligence, actual malice or gross irresponsibility in airing the story.

Fortunately, when you or your station is sued for libel there are specific legal defenses. It's important to know these defenses, particularly in an age when just about anyone can sue anybody, including news producers.

WARNING! BAD CALLS

Local television stations and cable channels faced a number of difficult ethical dilemmas during the last two years. These stories ranged from the live broadcast of a Los Angeles freeway suicide, a hidden-camera video of sex acts, to school shootings in several states. These and other questionable decisions further embarrassed local television news, already under attack for sensational coverage and too much crime news. At some point in each story, producers were involved. These bad calls could have been avoided if a producer had asked some ethical questions.

TIP
DEFAMATION LAWS VARY

The only national standard for libel regards public figures, otherwise libel or defamation depends on state laws, which vary. For example, some have different standards for a private person. It behooves you to know the law in your state or states if your market crosses state lines.

126

POWER PRODUCER: A PRACTICAL GUIDE TO TV NEWS PRODUCING

Defense against libel: the truth. To avoid a libel judgment against you, the best defense is that the story is accurate and true. Sounds simple, but you need to be able to prove truth in court. A judge or a jury, not your newsroom colleagues, will decide whether the facts back up the story. You need solid details backed by proper documentation and reliable sources.

Defense against libel: reporter's privilege. Remarks, comments or charges made in a legislative body like Congress or in an open court are considered privileged and may be reported. You may also report information from government documents such as a police report or an audit. Of course you must report these statements accurately and fairly in order to avoid libel.

Defense against libel: fair comment. You may provide opinion or commentary on a person or group that seeks public approval such as a sports team, a restaurant or a theater performance. However, you may only comment on the quality of the performance. You can't make outrageous statements that aren't true. For instance, you can say a football team played poorly but you can't attribute the quality of play to the team taking bribes, unless you have proof that will stand up in a trial.

Libel and public figures. Someone who courts fame or seeks a public office loses some of his or her ability to actually win a libel suit. This is the basis for the famous *New York Times v. Sullivan* case that involved an elected official in Alabama. Montgomery Public Safety Commissioner L.B. Sullivan sued the *Times* for libel but lost in the U.S. Supreme Court. This ruling held the plaintiff, as a public figure, must demonstrate "actual malice" or "reckless disregard for the truth" on the part of the news organization. These are harder to prove than negligence or gross irresponsibility.

Retractions. While not a defense, a retraction can help when someone is angry at your station for an inaccurate story. Stations run retractions because someone who feels they were wronged asked for a retraction and your lawyers think this will mitigate damages if there is a lawsuit. As a producer, you'll find yourself inserting a retraction statement in your newscast. Usually the station lawyers or the news director writes the retraction. Needless to say, you can't pull a retraction because sports ran over!

Privacy Law

Closely related to libel law, privacy law is based on the idea that private people have a right to redress if their personal privacy is violated in some way by your station or you as a producer. Privacy law includes issues like revealing private information, invading private property and generally putting someone in what is termed "false light."

Appropriation or commercialization. Privacy cases include misappropriation of someone's likeness, usually for commercial purposes. While news coverage is considered exempt from misappropriation because the individual was involved in a news story, this is not the case with advertising, including news promos. For instance, one station used a woman in a bikini as part of a news series on cruise ships and then used the same tape in a promo. She threatened legal action claiming the video held her up to ridicule. She received a settlement because she complained about a promo, not the news series.

False light and file tape. False light means showing someone in a negative aspect. For instance, sloppy use of file tape can cause big problems. In one case a station used file tape of people drinking in a bar to illustrate a story on alcoholism. One person in the tape sued. To make matters worse, the tape had been used in previous newscasts and when the man complained the station promised it wouldn't be used again. Allowing a tape editor or intern to pull file tape to illustrate a sensitive story can create a privacy lawsuit. As a

---

WARNING! BUZZWORDS

As a broadcast news writer, you can unintentionally commit libel through sloppy language. Certain buzzwords used in connection with someone's name or picture in a story can involve you in a libel suit. What are these words? Try rapist, sexual predator, thief, robber, embezzler, drug dealer, or other names used in news copy. Also remember that the word "alleged" really can't get you off the hook. You must have clear attribution from a responsible source for any facts included in a story.

TIP: ACTUAL MALICE

To prove actual malice the plaintiff must prove that the station aired the story knowing it was false, or that it recklessly disregarded the truth. In other words, the station ignored information it had that would have disproved or weakened the story, and aired it anyway.

producer, always look at the file tape of any story involving any issue that could put someone in a false light.

Private information. Another potential lawsuit is when your newscast reveals, without permission, private information about someone when there isn't any news value to the information. For example, your station for no apparent reason reports a private citizen has HIV or AIDS. Don't publish private facts if the information is highly offensive to that private citizen and there is no legitimate public interest.

Paparazzi laws. The irritating activities of tabloid photographers were considered more an ethical than legal issue, but so-called paparazzi laws demonstrate that privacy law is still evolving. Laws designed to protect individuals' privacy have increased since the death of Princess Di because of tabloid photographers. More and more bills are being introduced to curb intrusive media. Only the most recent are paparazzi laws, enacted in California, to limit the rights of photographers.

Private property. If your camera crew hasn't asked you about public access, it will soon. The type of privacy case you deal with most often is going on private property to tape a story. You can go on private property, without prior consent, only for a newsworthy reason, such as a plane crash. However, police can restrict that crew's movements in an emergency. They have to leave if asked to do so by the property owner. Whether you are on private property or not, local laws and police rules govern the access you can have to the scene of an emergency. You need to know the local laws because not all law enforcement officers know them or are willing to give a crew access to the scene of a story. You may have to negotiate.

Public vs. private property. What was once considered routine, like accompanying police on a raid, is an increasing legal problem. The courts don't like news crews doing this to get a story and see it as an invasion of privacy. CBS News lost a case in New York City in which a news crew was invited on a drug raid and entered an apartment with officers. There were no drugs, the story never aired, but the family sued CBS and won. Think twice before going on a police raid on private property. Legally, it is permissible to photograph or interview people for a news story without their permission as long as you are on public property such as a street or sidewalk. You normally need an invitation or prior consent when going on private property.

The debate over access gets heated when you start trying to cover stories at shopping malls. Malls have replaced the downtown business district as the place where people congregate. They are the best places to go if you need public reaction to a big story or need interviews. However, when sending a crew to a mall, it's a good idea to get prior approval. Most malls don't like camera crews. Whether a mall is considered a public or private place depends on your state.

Because laws vary widely from state to state, get yourself up to speed on your state's laws as quickly as possible. For instance, some states require both parties' consent to make a tape recording of a telephone conversation; others have laws regarding the use of hidden cameras; and some have shield laws that give journalists limited privilege to withhold the names of confidential sources.

Freedom of Information. Beyond libel and privacy, you will encounter a number of other legal issues such as Freedom of Information and copyright laws. Once again, learn these laws. If you work as a producer on a major investigation, you may well need to file a Freedom of Information request to get at important governmental papers. Before making an FOI request, clear it with the news director. She needs to know because if it's turned down you may have to go to court.

Copyright. If you want to use a clip from a movie, television program or any other copyrighted material in your newscast, think twice. The studios provides clips, called trailers, for movie reviews, but using part of a movie in a story is different. You have to obtain permission from the copyright owner before you can use the material. You may get a nasty letter from a movie studio demanding a hefty rights payment.

Your Ethical Foundation

The laws covering libel and privacy are designed to provide redress for the worst sins of journalists. However, ethics is different. Ethics covers everything you do as a journalist. It is about doing the right thing, and providing news and information your viewers can trust. At the same time, ethics is about protecting your professional integrity and the credibility of your newsroom.

The burden and responsibility for good judgment is on you as a producer. This is the reason power producers develop a personal code of ethics. The best journalistic ethics start with individual values and a sense of responsibility to the public. Use this code as a framework for making sound decisions.

For young and relatively inexperienced producers, it is sometimes difficult to keep an ethical compass. The pressure for ratings can drive some people to make thoughtless decisions. Certainly the speed with which information and video travels, the proliferation of live satellite feeds and live helicopter shots, makes it imperative you develop standards for making quick calls.

One way of looking at ethics is to follow the golden rule: Do unto others as you would have them do unto you. You don't want to do harm through thoughtless coverage. Unfortunately, most ethical issues aren't simple. There is a good deal of gray in ethics.

A good place to start as you formulate your own personal professional ethical framework is the RTNDA Code of Ethics (below).

Of course there are other professional codes, including those from the Society of Professional Journalists (SPJ) and the National Press Photographers Association (NPPA). These codes are also well worth reading and incorporating into your own personal ethical framework.

Accuracy. At the heart of journalism ethics is accuracy. A journalist gets the information right. At the very least, start with minor concepts such as getting names spelled and pronounced correctly. How do you think viewers react when they see a well-known name misspelled or a name pronounced improperly? If you or your team can't get a name right, how can the audience believe a complicated story?

Fairness and balance. It's not enough to get the facts of a story, you also have to present the story so it makes sense and is fair to all

RTNDA CODE OF ETHICS

The responsibility of radio and television journalists is to gather and report information of importance and interest to the public accurately, honestly and impartially.

The members of the Radio-Television News Directors Association accept these standards and will:

1. Strive to present the source or nature of broadcast news material in a way that is balanced, accurate and fair.

A. They will evaluate information solely on its merits as news, rejecting sensationalism or misleading emphasis in any form.

B. They will guard against using audio or video material in a way that deceives the audience.

C. They will not mislead the public by presenting as spontaneous news any material that is staged or rehearsed.

D. They will identify people by race, creed, nationality or prior status only when it is relevant.

E. They will clearly label opinion and commentary.

F. They will promptly acknowledge and correct errors.

2. Strive to conduct themselves in a manner that protects them from conflicts of interest, real or perceived. They will decline gifts or favors that would influence or appear to influence their judgment.

3. Respect the dignity, privacy and wellbeing of people with whom they deal.

4. Recognize the need to protect confidential sources. They will promise confidentiality only with the intention of keeping that promise.

5. Respect everyone's right to a fair trial.

6. Broadcast the private transmissions of other broadcasters only with permission.

7. Actively encourage observance of this code by all journalists, whether members of the Radio-Television News Directors Association or not.

The RTNDA Board of Directors unanimously adopted this code on August 31, 1987.

involved. In other words, if you cover the views of only one side in a story, you aren't fair. An example is doing a story on an anti-abortion sit-in without hearing from pro-choice advocates. Stories without context and perspective aren't good reporting, and they don't serve the audience.

Objectivity. The best way to report a story objectively is to make sure it is accurate, fair and free of personal bias. People have a right to expect their news untainted by your personal interests or views. Power producers carefully look at their own attitudes and try to be even-handed.

Conflict of interest. Power producers avoid any situation that may create a possible conflict of interest. This is why you must be vigilant in dealing with those who have a stake in the way a story is reported. There are several ways you can give the appearance of a conflict of interest.

For example, it's a conflict to work part time for an organization that's in the news, including a non-profit. Another conflict is volunteering for a community organization that takes a position on local issues like school reform. Involvement in politics, at any level, with or without party affiliation, is an absolute conflict.

Taking gifts, called freebies, can also be seen as a conflict of interest. Say a local orchard sends the newsroom a basket of apples after you do a story on that orchard. Should you accept the gift? Purists would argue no. But your station probably has a specific policy on free trips, meals, tickets or gifts. They usually limit the dollar value of a gift you may accept. The best policy is to not accept anything of any value from a news source. Again, do nothing that can appear to sway your news judgment.

Reenactments and staging. Reenactments and staging are two ethical issues related in some ways because both involve videography. You probably have seen events, such as crimes, reenacted to help illustrate a story with only limited video. Such reenactments are used frequently on the tabloid news. Even network news does reenactments at times. However, most responsible news organizations restrict reenactments and require they be clearly labeled.

Staging means asking someone to do something specifically so you can photograph the action to illustrate a story. The best way to deal with staging is to be up front with the viewers and tell them in the script that this action was done for the cameras. The infamous NBC Dateline case where a crew used a sparking device to help a truck's gas tank blow up was a case of staging. They made a bad decision when viewers were not told about the sparking device.

Identification of video news releases. At one time there was a policy that video supplied by an outside, non-news organization should be identified by a super. This policy is no longer followed religiously. It should be, because the public needs to know when part of the newscast comes from a source with a special interest. Most of this tape is innocuous, such as clips of horse races supplied by the tracks or business video of a new product like a car. Still, integrity in news means being honest with viewers.

Hidden cameras. As a producer you may be involved in a story using hidden cameras. Before getting involved, make sure station policy on using hidden cameras is followed and that the news director has approved it. Undercover work can be an invasion of privacy and your station can be sued for the manner in which the story was gathered.

News Smarts

Developing news smarts is the best way to avoid legal and ethical tangles. News smarts is a body of practical wisdom that power producers learn. It means having the experience and knowledge you need to know what kinds of stories cause problems. What follows are only a few of the most important things you need to know.

Station policy. As soon as you arrive at a new newsroom, get a copy of your station's news policy manual. This policy should cover potential issues you might face, including identification of accident or crime victims, the use of hidden cameras, and retractions. It's almost impossible for a station policy manual to cover every possible question, but it's a good starting point. In particular, the policy manual should make clear who has the final word on airing a risky story. Without a news manual, your best bet is to sit down with the news director and get a clear sense of all the unwritten policies that exist in that newsroom. Get specific guidance on how to handle a problem story and whom to call in a crisis.

Criminal identification. This is an area that should be covered by station policy. Stations shouldn't identify minors under a certain age when they will be tried as a minor in the juvenile justice system. Just who is considered a minor varies by state. However, this rule is being questioned thanks to the school shootings and other violent crime involving minors. Know your station policy and state's laws. Only identify minors with the approval of your news director.

Victim identification. Generally television news is careful about identification of crime victims. But the rules are changing as in the ban on identification of rape and sexual assault victims. Until the William Kennedy Smith rape case in Florida, the names of victims were not reported. In that case NBC News and several major newspapers identified the victim. Subsequently, some states, including Florida, passed legislation to bar media from naming victims. However, other rape victims say they don't mind being identified and want to speak out. This is a tricky issue, so clear any victim identification with your news director.

Offensive video. It's sometimes difficult to keep your head about you in covering breaking news. Today you're bombarded by video images from feeds, from your photographers and from your station's live helicopter. It's easy for you to overlook disturbing video that needs to be cleared by news management. A recent example was the Michigan couple who saw videotape of their daughter being tortured. The tape had been shown in a California trial of the man charged with her murder. A producer didn't think through the implications of the video and wasn't aware that it involved a local woman. A power producer would have reviewed the tape and thought twice before using it.

Suicides. An unwritten rule in television news holds that you don't report suicides. This rule does get broken. For instance, a highly public suicide can become news, like someone jumping from the fourth story of a mall atrium in front of thousands of shoppers. Always check with news management before using a suicide story. There must be sound news value to report a suicide.

> **WARNING! PROTECT ANONYMITY**
>
> When crime victims or other news sources agree to be interviewed but only on condition of anonymity, make sure they stay anonymous. In the rush to air, despite promises to alter their voice and not show their face on camera, stations have failed to protect these interviewees. Use the utmost care in handling such an interview and don't rush to get it on the air.

Scanners and tips. Don't report a story as fact based on only a scanner or tip. Take the time to get the facts and confirm the information with known sources. Television newsrooms have been the targets of elaborate hoaxes. A famous case involved then Washington Mayor Marion Barry, and a telephone tip to a newsroom that he had been shot near his home. At least two stations went on the air without proper confirmation. He hadn't been shot and wasn't near the neighborhood. Everyone involved was humiliated in the national media. Get it first, but first get it right.

Off the record. Today, most stations will allow an interviewee to go off the record to get background information on a story. The problem can come if you obtain good information on an important story that can't be confirmed by another source. At this point, using the material is not up to you. Discuss the story with your news director.

Sources. Sources who refuse to be identified are a problem, particularly in television where you are expected to have pictures of a person being interviewed. However, stations and networks do use unidentified sources. This was certainly true during the Clinton-Lewinsky scandal. But always remember that one of the major and repeated criticisms of local television news is a lack of clearly identified sources in many stories. Also, be sure to follow the accepted rule that there must be two reliable sources for a complex or investigative story with at least one source identified.

Embargoes. Major announcements, business, political and otherwise, are frequently issued as a news release with a time embargo. Public relations people do this to give all news media in a market an even playing field. But sometimes they try to preserve a big story for the morning newspaper. Television newsrooms take the position that they can report the story, despite the morning embargo, on their late newscasts. This is the time most major morning papers put out their first edition.

Red flags. With news smarts, power producers know certain subjects need to be treated carefully because they have the potential to become a problem. There is one overriding rule: If you have to ask if something is all right to air, then it probably isn't!

■ Stories involving sex or nudity always present a potential difficulty. You might offend some people by the discussion of sex unless the story is done with care and adequate warnings.

■ In television news, nudity can only be hinted at tastefully, such as a bare back. Always review the tape for any story involving sex or nudity.

■ Profanity also offends the public. The same rule applies. Review the tape before air. When a sound bite is absolutely essential, then beep out the profanity. When in doubt, check with your news director.

■ Violent or tasteless video, the face of a murder victim, blood on the street, or a sobbing relative, offends most viewers. They don't want to see their dinner interrupted by disquieting pictures. If you feel you must show it, warn the audience that they are going to see something unpleasant. In the case of the suicide shown live in Los Angeles, the coverage was even more offensive because the news departments broke in during children's programming.

■ Crime and court stories may offer good daily fodder for local news, but they involve a high risk of libel or privacy suits. Always review these scripts for clear attribution. Carefully look

Interview: Television News Ethics

Robert Steele
*Associate Dean
Director, Media Ethics
The Poynter Institute
St. Petersburg, FL*

Bob Steele worked 10 years in television news as a reporter, executive producer and news director for stations in Iowa and Maine. He taught reporting, ethics and media law at the University of Maine before joining The Poynter Institute in 1989. He conducts research for newspapers and television stations and newsroom workshops on ethics and newsroom leadership. He is co-author of *Doing Ethics in Journalism* and works extensively with RTNDA.

In your workshops, what are the most frequently asked questions from news producers?

The question of graphic video comes up over and over. How do we handle tape that shows a tragedy unfolding, a victim in agony, family members reacting to tragedy, or dead bodies and human beings injured in natural disasters?

Also, I get questions on the authenticity of information. How do we know that what we are getting on the feed is factually accurate and contextually authentic when we don't have either the time or means to check it out? Frankly, I wish this question would come up more because I think a lot of times producers don't even ask about verification.

Fairness and balance of coverage come up when it's a breaking story. How do you get and report the other sides of an issue when facing a deadline? These stories might deal with political controversy, allegations of wrongdoing or special interest groups making accusations against someone. These are a few of the issues.

What do you tell producers about dealing with graphic video?

I call upon the principle of truth telling. It's the paramount responsibility. It's the duty of journalists

at the way people are identified. Identifying someone improperly, such as convicting them on television, before the jury has decided, can be a bonanza for lawyers.

Law and ethics are complicated but critically important. This chapter got you off to a good start learning what you need to know. But remember, both subjects demand life-long study because of new ethical dilemmas and the constant change in the law. Fortunately, organizations like RTNDA and The Poynter Institute offer good information. *Communicator*, RTNDA's monthly magazine, includes a monthly legal column; other broadcast trade publications also report on changes in the law.

Try to attend one of the ethics workshops organized by RTNDA, the Freedom Forum or the Poynter Institute. SPJ sponsored an excellent book called *Doing Ethics in Journalism*, by Jay Black, Bob Steele and Ralph Barney. This invaluable resource is now in its third edition. Of course, Shoptalk features lively debates on all kinds of ethical issues.

Knowing and mastering all seven roles of a power producer isn't enough. You can stay out of legal trouble, write great copy and brilliant teases, build a powerful team, and be an incredible journalist, but all this might not help if you work at an understaffed and poorly equipped station. You've got to be equally smart about developing your career. Making intelligent career choices is covered in the next chapter.

---

to reveal meaningful information about significant issues and events in a thoughtful and professional way.

This principle has some tension with the principle of minimizing harm, particularly when you're reporting on tragedy or viewing stories that have graphic video with the potential to harm people. What I suggest is to recognize these principles and accomplish both truth telling and minimizing harm.

One suggestion I offer is to front-end stories as much as possible. If you know you have a feed or tape from a crew with graphic images, then start talking about it early. If you have a chance, talk over how to shoot it beforehand. Secondly, if you can't control the way it's shot, then look at different ways you can tell the story not only with the visual images but with the words.

The third point is to talk about tone and degree. How might you use graphic video while minimizing harm? It might mean not using that video in a cold open or a tease. Or, you may actually use more of the video but within a package that offers context on the larger scene. Make the video a piece of a mosaic that shows something much larger than a body or grieving relative.

What would you recommend producers do when they feel there are serious ethical questions about directions from their news managers?

There are a couple of things. One is to have clarity on your own principles and values. Know what you stand for, even in those cases where it's different from what your manager might stand for. Be aware of your own beliefs and biases.

Don't look at ethical decisions as two polar opposites of just black and white choices. Ethics is more complex and there is a lot of gray. Recognize the conflict and search for common ground. It's not to say give up your principles, but recognize other people also have legitimate values.

In recognizing competing values and principles, be good at articulating what it is you stand for so that you can make a strong case with your manager. Be clear, cogent, thoughtful and courageous in making a strong argument for what you believe.

It goes back to the old notion that the boss wants you to come up with solutions, not problems. If you have an ethical concern as a producer, don't go in and just make your argument. Don't just say, "No, I'm not going to do it." Instead say, "Here are my concerns, here is why I have these concerns, and let me suggest a couple of alternatives we can use to resolve this and still honor the principles of truth telling."

What is the best way for somebody just starting out as a production assistant or entry-level producer to develop a set of ethical principles?

There is no one way to do it. I would suggest producers spend time with reporters and photographers when they're in the field or in the edit bay. Ask good questions. "Tell me what's on your mind. Tell me your thoughts about this issue." Input from others helps us refine and form our own values and principles. It also gives us a better level of mutual understanding and a common ground in which we can then talk through tension and even significant disagreement.

For instance, a veteran photojournalist may be opposed to talking with family members of victims because at one time in his or her career a profoundly significant experience may have created that position. Understanding that feeling may help a producer talk to the photojournalist and ask that person to consider, in this situation, talking to the family members in a thoughtful and compassionate way. If the producer and photojournalist start at opposite ends of the spectrum, and it becomes a "You'll do it" "No I won't do it" standoff, then the interview is not going to happen.

In many shops there's deep animosity between crews in the field and the folks inside. It's ironic because in television we do work in teams, much more than newspaper people. This animosity and lack of understanding erode teamwork.

Are there any particular types of stories producers should be alert to, the kinds of stories that can pop up and cause trouble?

I think video news releases are something we need to be cautious about. Make sure a VNR provides an honest element to the reporting. Also, properly and consistently identify VNR material for your viewers.

Another area producers should pay more attention to is diversity within reporting. Try to bring a range of voices and perspectives into stories that meaningfully reflect your community and the diversity of our larger society. Whom do we select as sources on stories? Whom do we talk to when we do any kind of reaction to issues or breaking stories?

All too often when I look at tapes from stations before a workshop, I don't see an honest portrayal of the community in terms of its many shades of color, age and socioeconomic status. This is true in routine coverage, whether about elections, Christmas shopping or digging out from a storm.

As journalists, we gravitate to what and whom we know. Journalists tend to be in higher socioeconomic levels, and whiter and younger than the general population. I believe that leads us into a narrower band of selection of story ideas and sound. Producers can help not only in the selection process but also in the morning and afternoon meetings by asking questions about where stories are going to be shot and who is going to be interviewed.

One of the most difficult things for a producer is that you are trapped inside a building. I think producers, by their own choice, should find ways to spend time in their communities. They should at least break away from lunch at McDonalds or Subway and go to a Vietnamese restaurant or a Hungarian restaurant. See what's happening in different parts and cultures of our community. Drive to work different ways. Go through different neighborhoods and see what's going on. Go to a mall or a little league baseball field and sit and talk to people. Hear what they have to say.

One of the most important things we can do as journalists is be curious and ask good questions. That allows us to be smarter. And the best producers are the ones who are not only very good at television but also knowledgeable about their communities and the issues of the community and society. They can suggest meaningful approaches to covering issues and events in more significant and meaningful ways.

Listen for the unfamiliar, search for the uncomfortable. Then connect what you learn about your community to your station's news coverage.

Chapter 16

You & Your Career

In This Chapter:

- Do You Have What It Takes?
- Getting a Job and Moving Up
- Your Career
- When Things Don't Go Well
- Keeping Your Career Fresh

Chapter 16: You & Your Career

> "In your job hunt you can't be satisfied with anything less than an exceptional effort."

You see letters in Shoptalk from people who complain they can't get a producing job despite years of experience. On the other hand, you read about a 28-year-old producer with five years in television news appointed to a major newscast in a large market. While that young producer works to achieve clear career goals, the frustrated person may never have set any specific goals and won't rise above the skills of a mechanic. Where your career takes you certainly depends on your producing skills, but also on developing your career.

This chapter, on developing a successful career, starts by asking you some tough questions. First, do you have the personality, professional skills and personal drive of a power producer? Once you know if you are producer material, then this chapter covers how you get a job, particularly that first producing job. Then you learn how to set career goals and how to plot your professional life. You'll also receive valuable tips on what to do when you get fired. Finally, you'll learn how to keep your skills fresh so you don't slip back into being a journeyperson producer.

Do You Have What It Takes?

If you are thinking about a career, as a show or field producer, you should understand these aren't jobs for everyone. If you are already producing, you know the job takes a unique person. Beyond professional skills, you need to consider your value system, personality and psychological makeup. Test yourself. Do you like being in charge? Do you like working with others to accomplish a task? Are you organized? Probably the most important question is what do you need for a sense of accomplishment? Before making a final commitment to a producing career these are basic questions you want answered.

If you aren't yet producing, but think it looks like an attractive career, here are three suggestions on ways to evaluate the job.

Secure an internship. If you're still in college, find a newsroom internship and get yourself assigned to work with a producer. If you are already out of school, stations can't allow you to do an internship for legal and insurance reasons, but there are some options. For example, you can shadow a producer for a day or two, and ask questions about his job.

Get a part-time job. One way to learn if producing suits you is to take a part-time production or desk assistant's job in a station or cable newsroom. You'll work with producers on newscast production. These positions turn over rapidly, so even if nothing is available in the market now, keep trying. If you enjoy the work, production assistants are often promoted to producing in medium and small markets. Show your interest in producing by volunteering to produce during holidays and vacations.

Go to a small market. Small-market stations regularly hire entry-level people to do both reporting and producing. This is a great way to test both jobs and to find out which is most rewarding for you.

Getting a Job and Moving Up

Once you've decided you want to be a producer, or if you are already working as a producer but want to move up, landing a job is a job. Finding the right job requires time and dedication. You'll need organization, diligence and salesmanship to land a good producing job. In your job hunt you can't be satisfied with anything less than an exceptional effort. Here are some tips.

Create a great resume. Make a resume using one of the standard templates found in your

---

> **TIP**
> **TAKE A TEST**
>
>
> One way to see if you are suited for producing is to take a Myers-Briggs Type Indicator test. This test tells you a good deal about who you are, your personal and work style, and how you work with other people. Most colleges and many private psychologists can administer this test.

word processor and follow the advice in one of the resume books you find at most major bookstores. In creating your resume, right after your name and address, it's important to state that your career goal is to become a producer or, if you are already producing, produce a more important broadcast. When news directors see you're interested in producing they'll look at your resume. They're always hunting for producers.

Compile a tape. If you aren't yet producing newscasts, you won't have a tape of a newscast. But you can land a job based on writing samples and a statement of news philosophy. During your job interview, though, be prepared to lay out a practice newscast.

If you are already producing, send a complete newscast, minus commercials. Don't send a tape of election night coverage or a huge story. News directors want to see how you handle routine news days. Be prepared for a call asking you to send the previous night's show or today's newscast.

Save your best scripts. News directors want to see writing samples from your newscast or broadcast newswriting class. Save some of your best newswriting and include copies with your application.

Learn how to network. Networking offers an excellent way to find a job for producers and those just entering television news. You meet valuable people at events like the annual RTNDA conference and regional conferences. The annual conference includes a student track with panels on finding a job and a place for posting resumes. If you're a minority, consider joining one of the national groups like the National Association of Black Journalists (NABJ) or the Asian American Journalists Association (AAJA). These groups hold yearly conferences attended by many of the major broadcast groups and all of the television news headhunters.

Arrange informational interviews. If you're interested in working in a particular part of the country or in a specific city, invest in a trip to do informational interviews with news directors or executive producers in that region. Don't even ask for a job! Find out what they look for in a producer and what kind of experience you need to work in their newsroom. Ask other questions, like which smaller stations or cable operations do they respect and what markets do they consider when looking for a producer. Afterwards, let the news director know where you landed. Then stay in touch.

Look for openings. Concentrate your job search on actual job openings. You find these openings from a variety of sources, and they are listed at the end of this handbook in the appendix. When you find a desirable opening, don't hesitate. Mail your resume along with any material requested in the job listing. The quickest way to lose out on getting a job interview is a cover letter with misspellings, bad grammar and mistakes like getting the news director's name wrong. Double-check and proofread your cover letter and resume. Call to confirm the spelling of the news director's name.

Now you have to wait. It can take a news director a long time to select a list of finalists, particularly during a sweeps period. Don't be impatient and bug her. And don't call if the posting says no calls!

Make the most of the interview. Finding the opening and getting off a resume and tape are only the first steps. Next is the job interview. This step is actually more crucial than the resume and

---

TIP
DON'T BE AMBIVALENT

If you're answering an ad for a producer position, don't lie and say you really want to be a producer when in your heart you really want to be a reporter. News directors aren't interested in hiring someone as a producer who will start nagging them for a reporter's job. This drives news directors nuts.

WARNING!
SEND COPIES

Never send a news director the original of your work, like a tape or script. Protect the originals and always send copies. News directors are notorious for losing applicants' materials.

WARNING!
RESUME AND TAPE PACKAGING

With all the resumes and tapes a news director receives, you need to do something to package yours so it stands out, but don't do anything outrageous. A dayglow orange resume and tape box aren't a good idea. Use good taste and demonstrate a sense of graphic design, a desirable producer trait.

TIP
GET ORGANIZED

Tackle your search the same way you tackle your regular job. Set regular work hours, keep records of everyone you talk to, write down every lead, and set specific goals for yourself every day.

tape. No matter how strong your application and references, a bad interview will kill your chances.

To give a good interview, be prepared. Research the station and the market. Read the local newspaper. The web is terrific for this kind of research. You want the interviewers to know that you are good at getting up to speed on a local market. Also, try to watch several of the station's newscasts before the interview. Knowing what the newscasts look like can impress interviewers.

Before you go for the job interview, get an idea of the pay scale in the market. There are several places to get this information, including Professor Vernon Stone's studies posted on the University of Missouri School of Journalism web site. He includes links that give the cost of living for various markets. Also, RTNDA has salary information on its web site at www.rtnda.org, and Alice Main's Producer Page web site contains salary surveys.

In the interview news managers will look for certain traits. These might not be the traits you anticipate. They look for:
- Good work ethic
- Ability to handle pressure and crisis
- Willingness to take initiative in solving problems
- Writing skill
- Sound news judgment
- General knowledge
- Compatible news philosophy
- Positive mental attitude
- Ability to work with others
- Your general fit with the newsroom staff

During the interview try to be natural and confident. Also, this is a sale call; you're selling yourself. Be interested in the station and the job; don't hold back even if you have concerns about the newsroom or market. If you're asked to evaluate the newscast, be honest, but don't be harsh. If you see problems, offer solutions. Be prepared for a current-events and general knowledge quiz, and a writing test. Also, some stations may ask you to take a personality test.

Remember that a job interview gives you a chance to ask questions about the newsroom and the market. However, let them get their questions out of the way first. When you prepare your questions write down things you couldn't answer while researching the station and market. Also, talk to other people in the newsroom and ask them questions about the station. This is a chance to find out if you will fit in with the other people and the newsroom.

Learn how to evaluate a station. There are three main things to look at in evaluating a newsroom: equipment, staffing and ownership.

Does the station have good equipment and current technology? As a younger producer you need experience working with satellites and microwave live shots, CNN feeds, digital non-linear editing and digital video equipment. Television news is moving into a new digital phase so employers will be looking for producers who are skilled at using the latest technology.

Does the newsroom have enough people? An understaffed newsroom is a nightmare for producers. Also, will you be able to learn from the rest of the staff? Is there a power producer who might serve as a mentor? Is the newsroom a mix of knowledgeable veterans and well-trained younger people? Too many veterans or too many beginners in a newsroom can be difficult.

Staffing and equipment will depend in large measure on the station or channel's ownership. The whole culture of the station and newsroom is decided by the nature of the owner. This is also important because there is now a wide disparity in the kind of resources owners bring to a newsroom. Look for quality groups like Belo, Post Newsweek, Gannett or Hearst Argyle. These are

WARNING!
MARKET SIZE

Too many people in television news put too much importance on market size in evaluating a job. Market size isn't important; it's the quality of the newsroom. There are fabulous medium- and small-market newsrooms where you will learn a good deal. On the other hand, there are some awful stations in attractive markets where you won't learn a thing. Living in a great market is meaningless if you hate your job.

large and successful companies that can withstand a downturn in the economy. They also own a number of stations and you can advance from small-market stations to the largest markets within these groups.

Evaluate the job offer. When you get a job offer, you need to decide if this is the right job, the best situation, and one that serves your career needs. Make up your mind about a possible job based on solid reporting, not emotion. Talk again to people you met during the job interview. Find someone who worked at the station but has moved on, an excellent source of information. Go into the job with your eyes wide open.

Job offers can be negotiated. While the news director may be tough, it won't kill the deal if you ask for a little more money or more help with the cost of your move. There is usually some room in the news budget for a little better money.

Study the contract. Increasingly, news directors are asking producers to sign a contract. News directors want a contract because they are frustrated by the short tenure of young news producers. Faced with a contract, you should take a careful look at the provisions.

■ **Pay:** Your salary should be specified and it should go up in the second year. Look at the increase percentage and make sure you can live with the increase.

■ **Duties:** Are you assigned to a specific show? If your assignment changes then the contract should be renegotiated unless it specifies a new pay scale for a promotion.

■ **Outs:** You might be able to negotiate what's termed an "outs" clause that allows you to leave the station under certain circumstances, such as at the end of the first year or for an offer from larger markets. It's all negotiable.

Your Career

As your career progresses, drifting from job to job will only leave you frustrated and unsuccessful. The only way to succeed professionally and personally is to set goals for yourself. You have to decide what you want to accomplish. For instance, you may decide you want to be a line producer and then progress to executive producer. Perhaps your long-term goal is to be a news director by the time you're 40. Or you may start as a line producer but decide you want to be a special projects producer so you can make the jump to a network producer's job. These are reasonable goals and can be great careers.

If you enjoy producing broadcasts, you can actually work your entire career doing just that. It can be a rewarding life if you want to settle in one community. However, for most producers, line producing is the first major career step. You usually start as a noon or morning show producer and then move up to the more important programs. You can then progress to a good station in a major market. After that there are all kinds of different career possibilities for a power producer.

One option is news management. After several years of producing, your next career step could be to executive producer. Then the steps go through assistant news director to news director. Many news directors, particularly in larger markets, began their careers as line producers. To make more money and enjoy more responsibility, many producers aspire to become news directors.

Another career path from line producing is into field producing. Many field, special project or segment producers make the switch from line producing. Ultimately, these individuals can develop into network field producers who work with correspondents. Other options are story producers on magazine shows, or as segment producers on broadcasts like ABC Nightline or The Today Show.

When Things Don't Go Well

Every career, particularly in television, has bumps. When you feel pressure from news management or any of a thousand things management can do to make you uneasy, don't let it get out of hand. Deal with the situation. Ask the news director

---

WARNING!
GET PROMISES IN WRITING

Don't be so excited about a job offer or an impressive news director that you just sign the contract. Too many young and inexperienced producers have believed the news director when she said not to worry, that if you want to leave she will let you out of your contract. For one thing, that news director may be gone by the time you get a great job offer. Also, the news director may be a great person, but the station's general manager or lawyers may be bad news! Also, the contract may well include provisions that are unfair or unenforceable in your state. Don't be naive. Have a lawyer look at your contract.

what's wrong if you are feeling apprehensive about your job. Ask what you can do to better meet his goals and improve your relationship. If that doesn't work and you're unhappy in a job, don't just quit. It is better to look for a job when you have a job. Just be smart. Don't let them know you're looking.

Don't burn bridges. Television news is a small business. After awhile you discover everyone knows each other. This means you can't burn bridges. As much as you'd like to tell someone off, you must remember that in the future this person could hurt your career. For example, a news director is looking to fill a producer opening. You'd love to work in that newsroom, but after a great job interview you don't get the job. Little did you know that 10 years ago he worked with someone you don't get along with in your current job. He may well have gotten negative information about you from your newsroom antagonist and you'll never know.

What to do when you're fired. In television news, you can anticipate getting fired. However, if you are fired, it's not considered a black mark against you. Television news is subjective and everyone in the business knows it. There are dozens of different ways you can lose your job and news directors understand that it may have little to do with your performance.

When you are being fired, keep your wits about you. Now is the time to work out the best possible deal. If the news director offers a weak severance package, ask for a better deal. Most news directors feel bad when they fire someone. They may be willing to give you more than you think. More money will buy you more time to find the right job.

When you get fired, try to avoid getting too depressed. No, it isn't fun, but you will survive. Once you've gotten past the unpleasant shock, what you often find is you no longer fear being fired. You've become a stronger, more forceful producer. Always remember that it's common in television news for someone to get fired and wind up with a better job!

Keeping Your Career Fresh

Television allows little time to work on new skills and to keep your career fresh. The industry places little emphasis on training and career development. Some stations and cable news departments are getting better, but you have to take responsibility if you are going to keep your expertise sharp, learn new technology and develop the mastery required for a promotion or more challenging assignment.

Keep learning. Some companies provide training, particularly for management skills, but you also want to keep working on things like newswriting. Keep an eye out for opportunities and don't be shy about asking the news director to pay for you to attend a workshop or conference. The Poynter Institute offers producer and management workshops for broadcast journalists, as does RTNDA. Consulting firms, including Magid and AR&D, offer training for producers. The Broadcast Image Group has actually created a producer' school and offers regular classes.

View tapes. At times you can become so preoccupied with your own market that you forget stations elsewhere may be doing something new and unique. Keep yourself up to date by looking at tapes from other markets. You can get interesting tapes from your consultant or by contacting friends and relatives in other parts of the country.

Get feedback from consultants. Your station's news consultant should be helping you with producing. When consultants are in the newsroom, ask them for feedback on your show. Encourage your news director to get the consultant to conduct training sessions for producers.

Read to stay up to date. Reading industry publications and web pages is time well spent. Power producers stay on top of trends in the business. Every year or two reread one of the newswriting books. Doing so reminds you of the kind of writing you should be doing!

Conclusion

There are few careers more rewarding and more fun than television news producing. The future is only going to make producing more critical to the success or failure of a newsroom. The seven roles of a power producer won't change significantly as long as people rely on television or some form of television to get their news. And television news, by cable, satellite, or computer, is still the most powerful way yet devised to deliver information to the public.

Appendix

Resources for Producers

As a power producer, you can never stop learning about the television news business. You learn by constantly reading books and publications and visiting web sites devoted to some aspect of the craft. Also, many organizations offer training to help you advance your skills and career. What follows will get you going, but remember, there are new resources every week, particularly on the Internet.

Internet

While every organization and publication interested in journalism has a web site, the sites listed here are of particular interest to producers. You'll find these sites helpful in your work.

Shoptalk. Don Fitzpatrick compiles this daily e-mail listserv full of news about the television news business, people on the move, and spirited debate about issues. Virtually everyone in television news starts the day with Shoptalk. Distributed by Syracuse University, Shoptalk has more than 8,000 subscribers. To subscribe (or unsubscribe) to Shoptalk: Send an e-mail message to: listserv@listserv.syr.edu. In the body of the message, type subscribe Shoptalk, then put your real first name and real last name (all on the same first line). You can also find Shoptalk on the web site maintained by Don Fitzpatrick Associates. This site, www.tvspy.com, has an archive of past issues, job openings and a bulletin board for further debate on hot topics.

The Producer Newsletter. Alice Johnson Main edits and distributes a monthly e-mail newsletter for producers called The Producer Newsletter. The newsletter includes advice about producing, salary surveys, job listings and, my favorite, "I can't believe they said that," in which producers share the unscripted comments of their anchors. You can subscribe to this monthly newsletter by sending an e-mail to Main at ajmain@aol.com.

The Producer Page. This web site includes an archive of past issues as well as the valuable Producer Book, the best material from past monthly issues. It includes salary surveys as well as a great listing of web sites for producers. You can find The Producer Page at www.scripps.ohiou.edu/producer.

Medialine. Medialine is a subscription job service. Its web site includes daily news on the television news business as well as a bulletin board of questions about the business, mostly related to finding a job. The free information includes daily clips of news stories and promos, plus a daily profile of a job seeker with a little of his or her resume tape. The subscription job listing is the best place to look for a producing job. You'll find Medialine at www.medialine.com.

The Rundown. This weekly newsletter covers news series, special reports, new ideas and coverage of big stories. Your news director probably subscribes and with a little encouragement would probably be willing to distribute a copy to the producers. Editor and publisher Kim Standish has started a web site to complement the newsletter. You can look at some of the past issues at www.tvrundown.com. You'll also find helpful articles on issues like disaster coverage and writing, plus links to other sites.

University of Missouri. Professor Emeritus Vernon Stone has collected information on broadcast news salaries. You'll also find information on cost of living for various cities to help you with job decisions. See www.missouri.edu/~jourvs/gtvsal.html.

Audience Research and Development. This consulting firm has a valuable web site with good material on successful stations and industry trends. You'll find the site at www.ar-d.com. There is a link to Talent Dynamics, a sister firm, which does headhunting for client stations, and maintains a comprehensive job listing on its site. You'll find these jobs listings at www.talentdynamics.com.

RTNDA. RTNDA's web site includes information on RTNDA and RTNDF programs, workshops, publications, annual salary surveys and suggested coverage guidelines. Research studies on television news are also included. You'll find RTNDA at www.rtnda.org.

Books

Producing. There is only one other book on producing that you may find helpful.
■ *The Producing Strategy* by Larry M. Rickel and Ed Sardella. The book was self-published by the Broadcast Image Group. You can write The Producing Strategy, P.O. Box 6105, San Antonio, TX, 7820 9, or use the web site, www.broadcastimage.com .

Broadcast newswriting. The books by Ed Bliss and Mervin Block were written for professionals while the others are texts.
■ *Writing News for Broadcast* by Edward Bliss Jr. and James L. Hoyt. Columbia University Press, New York. 1994. ISBN: 0231079737. This is the third edition of the classic book by Ed Bliss who wrote at CBS News when broadcast newswriting was invented.
■ *Broadcast Newswriting: The RTNDA Reference Guide* by Mervin J.Block. RTNDA and Bonus Books, Chicago. 1994. ISBN: 156625017X. Block is another veteran network news writer and writes a regular newswriting column in *Communicator*.
■ *Writing Broadcast News. Shorter, Sharper, Stronger* by Mervin J. Block. Bonus Books, Chicago. 1997. ISBN: 1566250846.
■ *Writing News for TV and Radio: The Interactive CD and Handbook* by Mervin J. Block. Bonus Books, Chicago. 1999. ISBN: 1566251133.
■ *Broadcast News* by Mitchell Stephens. 3rd Edition. Harcourt Brace Jovanovich, College Publishers. Fort Worth, TX. 1997. ISBN: 0030791766.
■ *Broadcast News Writing, Reporting, and Producing* by Ted White. 2nd Edition. Focal Press, Boston. 1996. ISBN: 0240802454.
■ *Air Words: Writing for Broadcast News* by John Hewitt. 2nd Edition. Mayfield Publishing Company, Mountain View, CA. 1994. ISBN: 1559344377.
■ *Broadcast News Writing Stylebook* by Robert A. Papper. Allyn & Bacon, Needham, MA. 1994. ISBN: 0205146937.

Management. These books cover broader management issues particularly dealing with change, a constant in this business.
■ *Teaching the Elephant To Dance: The Manager's Guide To Empowering Change* by James A. Belasco. Crown Publishers, New York. 1991. ISBN: 0452266297.
■ *Leading Change* by John P. Kotter. Harvard Business School Press, Boston. 1996. ISBN:

0875847471.
- *Visionary Leadership: Creating a Compelling Sense of Direction for Your Organization* by Burt Nanus and Warren G. Bennis. Jossey-Bass Publishers, San Francisco. 1992. ISBN: 0787901148.
- *Managing Assertively: How To Improve Your People Skills* by Madelyn Burley-Allen. John Wiley & Sons, New York. 1995. ISBN: 0471039713.

Work types and styles. These three books are highly recommended for producers who want to know more about how to understand and relate to all the other people in the newsroom and station.
- *People Styles at Work: Making Bad Relationships Good and Good Relationships Better* by Robert Bolton and Dorothy Grover Bolton. AMACOM, New York. 1996. ISBN: 0814477232.
- *Work Types* by Jean M. Kummerow, Nancy J. Barger and Linda K. Kirby. Warner Books, New York. 1997. ISBN: 0446672173.
- *The Art of Speedreading People: Harness the Power of Personality Type and Create What You Want in Business and in Life* by Paul D. Tieger and Barbara Barron-Tieger. Little, Brown and Company, New York. 1998. ISBN: 0316845256.

People problems. These books have solid ideas for dealing with people who are hard to work with at times.
- *Coping With Difficult People* by Robert N. Bramson and Robert M. Bramson. Dell Publishing Company, New York. 1988. ISBN: 0440202019.
- *Dealing With People You Can't Stand: How to Bring Out the Best in People at Their Worst* by Rick Brinkman and Rick Kirschner. McGraw Hill, New York. 1994. ISBN: 0070078386.
- *Problem People at Work* by Marilyn Wheeler. St. Martin's Press, New York. 1995. ISBN: 0312131488.
- *The Complete Idiot's Guide to Getting Along With Difficult People* by Brandon Toropov. Alpha Books, New York. 1997. ISBN: 0028615972.

Coaching. These books will help you better understand the idea and process of coaching others on your team.
- *Coaching for Commitment : Interpersonal Strategies for Obtaining Superior Performance from Individuals and Teams* by Dennis C. Kinlaw. Jossey-Bass Publishers, San Francisco. 1999. ISBN: 0787939862.
- *Masterful Coaching: Extraordinary Results by Impacting People and the Way They Think and Work Together* by Robert Hargrove. Pfeiffer & Company, San Diego. 1995. ISBN: 0893842818.

Teams and conflict. These two books provide a basic understanding of how teams work and also how to resolve conflicts between team members.
- *Team Players and Teamwork: The New Competitive Business Strategy* by Glenn M. Parker. Jossey-Bass Publisher, San Francisco. 1996. ISBN: 0787901857.
- *Constructive Conflict Management : Managing To Make a Difference* by John Crawley. Nicholas Brealey Publishing, London. 1997. ISBN: 1857880145.

Office politics. This book takes the reader through lots of real-life examples of office politics and gives practical advice.
- *Winning Office Politics: Dubrin's Guide For the '90s* by Andrew Dubrin. Prentice Hall Press, Paramus, NJ. 1990. ISBN: 0139649581.

Reporting. If you have no experience in the field as a reporter or producer, you need to read these two books to learn more about field production and how reporters and photographers create news stories. Both will help you work with reporters.
- *Professional's TV News Handbook* by Charles Coates. Bonus Books, Chicago. 1994. ISBN: 1566250064.
- *Television Field Production and Reporting* by Frederick Shook. Addison-Wesley Publishing Company. 2000. ISBN: 0321044266.

Ethics. The following book is required for anyone wanting to know more about how to deal with ethical issues in journalism.
- *Doing Ethics in Journalism, A Handbook With Case Studies* by Jay Black, Bob Steele, Ralph D. Barney and the Society of Professional Journalists. Allyn & Bacon, Needham, MA. 1998. ISBN: 020528535X.

Personal goals. This is the classic for helping people get more direction and focus to their lives. You might not buy everything Covey says, but it will get you thinking about how to better achieve your goals.

■ *The 7 Habits of Highly Effective People* by Stephen R. Covey. Fireside, New York. 1990. ISBN: 0671708635.

Periodicals

Two major magazines cover the television industry and report on key issues in television news. Four other monthly magazines comment on issues in journalism including television news. Subscribe to at least one of the weekly magazines and one of the monthlies.

Broadcasting & Cable. This weekly magazine is strong in reporting on the news media, corporate changes and federal regulation. Also covers changes in technology such as DTV and the Internet. It does solid regular coverage of local television and in-depth stories on the major issues you'll be talking about around the water cooler in your newsroom. Excellent job listings. *Broadcast & Cable*, 245 West 17th Street, New York, NY 10011. Web: www.broadcastcable.com. To subscribe: 800.554.5729.

Electronic Media. Also a weekly, EM focuses on programming news, including developments in local television news. Also has good job listings. *Electronic Media*, 740 N. Rush St., Chicago, IL 60611.Web: www.emonline.com. To subscribe: 800.288.5900.

American Journalism Review. Published by the University of Maryland, AJR is strong on issues of news reporting and the business of journalism. Runs a regular column on issues in local television news. *American Journalism Review*, 1117 Journalism Building, University of Maryland, College Park, MD 20724. Web: www.ajr.org. To subscribe: 800.827.0771.

Brill's Content. Written for the general public, this monthly is less serious than AJR or CJR. B*rill's Content*, 521 Fifth Avenue, New York, NY 10175. Web: www.brillscontent.com. To subscribe: 800.829.9154.

Columbia Journalism Review. A bimonthly, CJR is mostly concerned with reporting and ethical issues involving print and television. *Columbia Journalism Review*, Journalism Building, 2950 Broadway, Columbia University, New York, NY 10027. Web: www.cjr.org. To subscribe: 888.425.7782.

Communicator. This monthly magazine from RTNDA contains information valuable to you as a producer and should be regular reading. It includes articles on new technology, management skills, newswriting, and the law, and practical information on trends in television news. You can get *Communicator* by joining RTNDA, which has affordable member rates for students and recent graduates. Call 800.80.RTNDA or see the web site at www.rtnda.org.

Training

Unfortunately, television news has a weak history of providing training for new or experienced producers. However, you do now have some opportunities to learn more about your chosen craft. These programs are valuable if for no other reason than you get to meet producers from other stations who face many of the same problems you face and who have come up with some answers. You'll learn that you are not alone!

The Poynter Institute. Provides seminars and workshops for broadcast reporters, producers, photographers and news managers. There are at least two five-day producer workshops each year. These workshops are a marvelous bargain since the cost includes the hotel room and some of your meals. You can get a current schedule by checking the web site at www.poynter.org. Poynter Institute, 801 Third Street South, St. Petersburg, FL 33701. Phone: 727.821.9494.

Television News Center. Run by broadcast news veteran Herb Brubaker, the center provides workshops for anchors, reporters and producers. Most of the programs last one day and include a guest instructor who is well-known in the field. You can get a schedule by calling or checking the web site at www.televisionnewscenter.org. Television News Center, 184 New Mark Esplanade, Rockville, MD 20850. Phone: 301.340.6160.

NewsLab. Former CBS and CNN correspondent Deborah Potter runs this nonprofit organization that tries to improve the quality of television news. Although she does workshops, Potter uses a hands-on approach to work with local stations on ways to improve reporting and producing. She also provides feedback on stories and suggests approaches for stories stations are planning. Contact the NewsLab for more on how it can help your newsroom, or check the web site at www.newslab.org. NewsLab, 1150 18th Street NW, Suite 775, Washington, DC 20036. Phone: 202.969.2543.

Radio and Television News Directors Foundation. RTNDF does at least one three-day producer workshop every year for women and minorities A nominal fee covers your hotel room and most meals. RTNDF also does workshops for women and minorities interested in news management, and a series of one-day regional workshops on issues like ethics and computer-assisted reporting. Check the RTNDA web site at www.rtnda.org for more details. RTNDF. 1000 Connecticut Ave., NW, Suite 615, Washington, DC 20036. Phone: 202.659.6510.

Consultants

The three largest news consulting firms all offer scheduled training for producers from clients stations. All are run by experienced broadcasters. You can find these opportunities by asking your news director or checking the firms' web sites or by talking with your station's consultant.

Frank N. Magid Associates. The Magid Institute™ provides training for news staff from client stations. Magid vice president Mackie Morris also conducts excellent writing seminars for stations and broadcast groups. Frank N. Magid Associates Inc., One Research Center, Marion, IA 52302. Phone: 319.377.7345. Web site: www.magid.com.

Broadcast Image Group. The Producing School at The Broadcast Image Group runs workshops for reporters, anchors, producers and news managers. It is run by former news director Paul Dughi. Broadcast Image Group, 7744 Broadway, Suite 100, San Antonio, TX 78209. Phone: 210.828.6664. Web site: www.broadcastimage.com.

Talent Dynamics. The headhunting subsidiary of Media Advisors International and AR&D offers regularly scheduled workshops on reporting, producing and management. Talent Dynamics, 8828 Stemmons, Dallas, TX 75247. Phone: 214.630.5097. Web site: www.talentdynamics.com.

Job Search

When you are looking for a job you will find numerous job listing sites on the Internet. There are also several fee-based sites. The two television weeklies—*Broadcasting & Cable* and *Electronic Media*—have job sections and list jobs on their web sites. Here are some places to look for jobs or to send your resume and tape.

Station and channel lists. Start your search by getting a complete list of stations and cable news operations. The most comprehensive is *The Broadcasting & Cable Yearbook*. You might be able to find a copy of this book in the reference section of your local library. Handy for station and channel telephone numbers is the AR&D *Little Black Book*. To get a copy call AR&D at 214.630.5097. The most useful and comprehensive list of stations is the NATPE *Station Listing Guide* issued each quarter. There is also a companion guide to group owners, broadcast and cable networks, and program distributors. It costs $35 per book for nonmembers. Call NATPE at 310.453.4440 or send an order to NATPE Publications Department, 2425 Olympic Blvd. Suite 550E, Santa Monica, CA. 90404. You can also find stations' web sites through www.ultimatetv.com or www.ajr.newslink.com.

TVspy.com. Don Fitzpatrick Associates in San Francisco maintains a comprehensive database of news people including producers. Job openings are regularly listed on www.tvspy.com.

The Producer Newsletter. Alice Main's e-mail newsletter lists openings each month. You can subscribe by e-mailing Main at ajmain@aol.com.

Talent Dynamics. Lists client job openings regularly on its web site, www.talentdynamics.com.

Broadcast Image Group. Lists client job openings for producers but isn't clear about which station or channel is looking. Check these listings at www.broadcastimage.com.

Frank N. Magid Associates. As this handbook is being written, Magid is revising its web site and does not currently list jobs. However, check www.magid.com to see if this large consulting firm is now providing job listings.

Periodicals. Both *Broadcasting & Cable* and *Electronic Media* have extensive job classified ads in each weekly issue. If you can't afford to subscribe, check your local community or college library for the current copy. Their web sites also list jobs, but charge a fee for this service.

Talent Shop. This new fee-based service is a joint venture of Medialine and Don Fitzpatrick Resources. Each candidate has a page complete with photo, resume and streaming video of their resume tape. This gives news directors the ability to see talent right at their desktop, without contending with piles of videotapes. Talent Shop also maintains a database of producer resumes. For more information, call 800.237.8073.

TV Jobs. Another fee-based web site. It has good listings but covers the entire television field, not just news positions. Web site: www.tvjobs.com.

Radio-Television News Directors Association. RTNDA members can access hundreds of current job listings on the members-only site at www.rtnda.org. Members also can post a brief description of their qualifications in a Talent Bank. For RTNDA membership information, see the web site or call 800.80.RTNDA.

Index

A

ABC, 47, 60, 121, 139
AIDS, 128
Abbreviations, 44, 87
Action News, 32, 54, 60
Advertisers, 116
Amburg, Van, 60
American Journalism Review, 144
American Meteorological Society, 77
American Movie Classics (AMC), 92
Anastos, Ernie, 60
Anchor, 17, 18, 23, 51, 60, 66, 69, 92, 96, 98, 102, 103-105, 108, 122
Animation, 17, 88
Appropriation, 127
Asian American Journalists Association (AAJA), 137
Assignment editor, 20, 32, 79
Associated Press, 33-34, 104
Attribution, 40
Audience, 17, 58, 93
Audience research, 116, 121-124
Audience Research & Development (AR&D), 28, 61, 120-121, 123, 140, 142, 145

B

Back-timing, 68-69
Banners, 86
Barnes & Noble, 28
Barney, Ralph, 133
Barry, Marion, 131
BASYS, 46
Beats, 34-35
Belfast, 42
Belo, 138
Beutel, Bill, 60
Bishop, Ann, 60
Black, Jay, 133
Bliss, Ed, 142
Block, Mervin, 142

Blocks, 52-55
Bonds, Bill, 60
Borders, 28
Boston Globe, The, 21
Brill's Content, 144
Broadcast Image Group, 58, 121, 140, 142, 145
Broadcast news writing, 39-47, 66, 142-143
Broadcasting & Cable, 120, 144-145
Bugs, 85
Bush, George, 82

C

CBS, 23, 34, 40, 58, 61, 85, 128, 142
CNN, 46, 92, 138
Capital Cities, 60
Central Intelligence Agency (CIA), 44
Character generators (CG), 72, 85
Chernomyrdin, Viktor, 45
Chriesman, Willie, 46-47
Clark, Michele, 23
Clichés, 42-44
Clinton, William, 21, 131
Coaching, 98-103, 143
Coast Guard, 26
Columbia Journalism Review, 144
Columbine High School, 36
Commercials, 65
Communication, 99-100, 113
Communicator, 133, 144, 145
Conflict of interest, 130
Consultants, 61, 140
Contracts, 139
Copyright, 128
Cost per point, 117
Crime victims, 131-132
Cronkite, Walter, 58
Cuba, 27, 28

D

Daly, Joel, 60

Demographics, 52, 58, 117-120
Designated Market Area (DMA), 26, 86, 89, 116-119
Diaries, 119-121
Difficult people, 108-114, 143
Director, 66-67, 70-72, 123-124
Disaster plan, 36-38
Doing Ethics in Journalism, 133
Dow Jones, 22

E
ESPN, 78, 92
Egad!, 85-88
Electronic Media, 144, 145
Electronic news gathering (ENG), 80-81
Embargoes, 131
Emmy Awards, 104
Enersen, Jean, 60
Engberg, Eric, 34
Enterprise reporting, 33, 50
Ethics, 17, 79, 128-134
Executive producer, 18, 69, 79, 108, 137
Eyewitness News, 54, 60

F
Fair comment, 127
False light, 127-128
Federal Aviation Administration (FAA), 22
Federal Communications Commission (FCC), 64
Finding, Hiring and Keeping the Best Employees, 102
Fitzpatrick, Don, 141, 145, 146
Flow, 54
Flynn, Fahey, 60
Focus groups, 122
Formats, 50, 59
Fox, 61
Franchises, 60, 78-79
Freedom Forum, 26, 133
Freedom of information (FOI), 128

G
Gallup Poll, 102
Gannett, 138
Gin, Janice, 8,16
Grammar, 45, 72
Grammar for Smart People, 22
Graphics, 37, 44, 67, 70, 72, 84-89
Grimsby, Roger, 60
Group W, 60

H
HIV, 128
Half, Robert, 102
Hard Copy, 61
Hearst Argyle, 138
Hidden cameras, 128, 130
Hill, Desiree Newhart, 123-124
Huntley-Brinkley Report, 58
Hutchings, Phil, 69-71

I
Inside Edition, 61
Internet, 22, 29, 141
Internship, 136
Interruptible feedback (IFB), 81
Interviews, 81-82
Investigative Reporters and Editors (IRE), 104
Investigative reports, 79

J
Jacobson, Natalie, 60
Jeopardy, 21
Job description, 13
Job search, 145
Journalist, 12, 15, 20, 84, 96

K
KARE-TV, 61
KCNC-TV, 46, 92
KGO-TV, 8, 16, 60
KHBS-TV, 123
KOCO-TV, 123
KOLR-TV, 123
KTRK-TV, 61
KTTV, 93
KTUL-TV, 23
KWTV, 123
Kaufman, Monica, 60
Kalodimos, Demetria, 104-105

L
Labels, 86
Latin America, 28
Leadership, 101-102
Leads, newscast, 50, 55
Leads, sentences, 40-41, 43-44
Lewinsky, Monica, 131
Libel, 126-127
Live reports, 80-81
Logos, 85

Los Angeles Times, 21
Lunden, Joan, 60

M

Macy's, 93
Magazines, 21-22
Magid, Frank N. and Associates, 61, 121, 140, 145
Main, Alice Johnson, 22, 23, 138, 141, 145
Management, 142
Maps, 29, 37, 86
Marchiano, Sal, 60
Market, 26
McHugh & Hoffman, 61
Medialine, 142, 146
Meters, 117-120
Metropolitan Statistical Area (MSA), 116-117
Murrow Awards, 104
Myers-Briggs Type Indicator, 102, 136

N

NBC, 58, 69, 85, 104, 121, 130, 131
National Association of Black Journalists (NABJ), 137
National Association of Television Programming Executives (NATPE), 120, 145
National Collegiate Athletic Association (NCAA), 76
National Press Photographers Association (NPPA), 129
National Public Radio (NPR), 22
National Transportation Safety Board (NTSB), 22
Natural sound, 95
New York Stock Exchange, 85
New York Times, The, 21, 34, 127
News conferences, 35
News director, 7, 79, 84, 108, 118, 123, 137, 139-140
News hole, 64-65
News releases, 35
News writers, 15, 17
News You Can Use, 60
NewsLab, 42, 144, 145
Newspapers, 21, 28, 34, 116
Newsweek, 21
Nielsen Media Research, 26, 27, 59, 79, 85, 114, 116-122
Nielsen Station Index (NSI), 116
Nightline, 139
North Atlantic Treaty Organization (NATO), 44
Northwestern University, 46

O

OPEC, 44
O'Donnell, Rosie, 58
Off the record, 131
Office politics, 109, 143
Over the shoulder box, 84-87
Overnights, 119

P

PBS, 27
Pace, 54
Paparazzi laws, 128
Papper, Robert A., 142
Penske, Roger, 98
Post Newsweek, 138
Potter, Deborah, 42
Power Producer Checklist, 73
PowerPoint, 122
Poynter Institute, The, 16, 36-37, 133, 140, 144
Price Cutter, 93
Primary Colors, 21
Primo, Al, 60
Princess Diana, 128
Privacy law, 127-128
Private property, 128
Producer Book, 23, 141
Producer Newsletter, 22, 23, 141, 145
Producer Page, 138, 141-142
Promotion, 15-16, 60, 79

Q

Q score, 121
Quantel Paintbox, 84

R

Radio, 22, 34
Radio and Television News Directors Foundation (RTNDF), 145
Radio-Television News Directors Association (RTNDA), 104, 129, 132-133, 137-138, 140, 142, 146
Rather, Dan, 40, 82
Ratings, 116-122
Read rate, 68
Reenactments, 130
Reporters, 13, 23, 32-33, 51, 66, 73, 80-81, 134
Reporting, 22, 20-24, 144
Resume, 136-137
Retractions, 127
Rickel, Larry, 58, 142

Rivera, Geraldo, 60
Rundown, 50, 65-66, 73
Rundown, The, 142

S

Sardella, Ed, 142
Satellite news gathering (SNG), 80-81
Scamardella, RoseAnn, 60
Scanners, 35, 131
Scripts, 69
Seinfeld, 121
Seven on Your Side, 60
Share, 117-118
Shoptalk, 136, 141
Simon and Schuster, 22
Sinatra, Frank, 21
Smith, William Kennedy, 131
Society of Professional Journalists (SPJ), 129, 133
Sony, 81
Sports, 53, 65, 67, 76-78, 121
Staging, 130
Standish, Kim, 142
Steele, Robert, 36-37, 132-134
Stephens, Mitchell, 142
Still store, 84
Stone, Vernon, 26, 28, 138, 142
Story count, 53-54
Story structure, 45
Suicides, 131
Sullivan, L.B., 127
Sweeps, 79-80, 118-121
Syracuse University, 9, 69, 141

T

Talent Dynamics, 142, 145
Talent Shop, 146
Tape, audition, 137
Tape editors, 66
Tape list, 70
Tarshis, Barry, 22
Team conflict, 113-114, 144
Team coverage, 36
Team leader, 15-16, 99-101, 108
Teams, 87, 98-103
Teases, 52, 88, 92-96, 118, 120
Telephone surveys, 122
TelePrompTer, 24
Television by Design, 88
Television households, 117
Television News Center, 144

Time, 21
Today Show, 139
Tracking studies, 122

U

Ultimatetv.com, 120
United Auto Workers (UAW), 44
United Press International (UPI), 34
University of Illinois, 104
University of Maine, 132
University of Missouri, 9, 26, 28, 34, 138, 142
University of Tulsa, 23
USA Today, 21, 34
U.S. News & World Report, 21

V

Valenta, Nancy, 93
Victim identification, 131
Video, 45, 51, 77, 95, 131, 133
Video news release (VNR), 35, 55, 130, 134
Viewers in Profile, 119
Voice-over, 68

WXYZ

WABC-TV, 60
WBBM-TV, 23
WBRC-TV, 46
WCCO-TV, 61
WCNC-TV, 92
WCPO-TV, 60
WCVB-TV, 46
WDIV-TV, 46, 69
WDSU-TV, 23
WICD-TV, 104
WJXT-TV, 77
WKRC-TV, 23
WLS-TV, 23, 46, 60
WPVI-TV, 32, 60
WSMV-TV, 104
WSVN-TV, 61
WVTM-TV, 46
WXYZ-TV, 60
Wall Street Journal, The, 21, 34
Washington Redskins, 27
Weather, 53, 65, 67, 69, 70, 76-77
Westinghouse, 60
Winfrey, Oprah, 58
Winterling, George, 77
Work types, 113, 143
Zindler, Marvin, 60-61

PN 1992 .75 .S56 2000 c.1

PN 1992 .75 .S56 2000 c.1